The Times

Of the Signs

Of the Revelation

William Wadsworth

William E. Wadsworth

Thank You

Special thanks to my wife and family for showing me how important relationships are to the Christian walk. My wife is also my translator. Understanding my thoughts about the Revelation would be impossible without her.

Love God, and love one another!

Acknowledgements

Thank you Ashley, my loving daughter for quickly turning my manuscript into this book!

Table of Contents

Foreword

The calendar for Israel's prophecies contains 12 months of 30 days which total 360 days/year. The 5 missing days each year are saved up for 6 years until an extra month of 30 days is added. This occurs in the same manner as an extra day is added every 4 years to our calendar during leap year.

The book of Daniel contains a prophecy about the last 7 years of Gentile rule over the people of Israel and the city of Jerusalem. Those 7 years or 85 months will begin with a covenant. The great tribulation will not begin at the start of the 7 years. It will start 42 months later when an abomination of desolation is erected. At this 42 month interval, 2 witnesses will lead the people of Israel into the wilderness for 1,260 days or another 42 months. During the last 3.5 days of this period, the 2 witnesses will be killed, and then raised from the dead with a great earthquake. This will end the period of great tribulation. The initial 7 years will last for another 30 days, at which time Jesus will begin his reign from a position above the earth. God's wrath, like Jesus' reign, will begin after the great tribulation. The start of God's wrath is not given, but it will be completed 75 days after the 2 witnesses are raised. Dan 12:12 says, "Blessed is he that waits and comes to the 1,335 days." (1,335 − 1,260 = 75) Blessed is he who survives the 1,260 days of great tribulation and the following 75 days which include the great wrath. The millennial kingdom awaits you!

The general sequence of the signs that prophesy the return of Jesus to earth is found in the seals of the Revelation and in the 24th chapter of Matthew. The 6th seal begins on the last day of the great tribulation. This seal moves away from generalizations to 5 specific signs. In order, the 5 signs are: A great earthquake, a sun, moon, star event, a vanishing sky, a visible heaven, and a period of wrath. The 2 most repeated elements of God's wrath are a second great earthquake and great hail. The great tribulation and/or at least one of these signs is associated with the events of Chapters 6, 7, 8, 11, 12, 13, 14, 15, 16, 17, 18, and 19. That is, the same signs will be seen again and again. Recognizing this cycle provides a breakthrough for understanding the timing of the events of the Revelation!

Chapter 1

1 The Revelation of Jesus Christ, which God gave unto him, to show unto his servants things which must shortly come to pass; and he sent and signified it by his angel unto his servant John:

2 Who bare record of the word of God, and of the testimony of Jesus Christ, and of all things that he saw.

3 Blessed is he that reads, and they that hear the words of this prophecy, and keep those things which are written therein: for the time is at hand.

4 John to the seven churches which are in Asia: Grace be unto you, and peace, from him which is, and which was, and which is to come; and from the seven Spirits which are before his throne;

The things that were to come "shortly" or were "at hand," were things about to occur, or events that were already in progress at the time John wrote the Revelation. Confidence in prophecies far into the future are made more sure when near term predictions come to pass. This is a common style among prophets. However, this is not to be confused with Jesus coming quickly. Jesus announces 6 times in the Revelation that he is coming quickly. Each time, he refers to the speed in which he will come once it is time for his return, not the length of time from the present.

It is interesting that the Holy Spirit is pictured as 7 Spirits.

5 And from Jesus Christ, who is the faithful witness, and the first begotten of the dead, and the prince of the kings of the earth. Unto him that loved us, and washed us from our sins in his own blood,

6 And has made us kings and priests unto God and his Father; to him be glory and dominion for ever and ever. Amen.

7 Behold, he comes with clouds; and every eye shall see him, and they also which pierced him: and all kindreds of the earth shall wail because of him. Even so. Amen.

We know from history that Jesus has still not been seen coming with the clouds. We can be confident that he will because of the accuracy of other prophecies. Signs leading to the quick return of Jesus will be the focal point of the Revelation from Chapter 6 through Chapter 19.

8 I am Alpha and Omega, the beginning and the ending, says the Lord, which is, and which was, and which is to come, the Almighty.

9 I John, who also am your brother, and companion in tribulation, and in the kingdom and patience of Jesus Christ, was in the isle that is called Patmos, for the word of God, and for the testimony of Jesus Christ.

10 I was in the Spirit on the Lord's day, and heard behind me a great voice, as of a trumpet,

11 Saying, I am Alpha and Omega, the first and the last: and, What you see, write in a book, and send it unto the seven churches which are in Asia; unto Ephesus, and unto Smyrna, and unto Pergamos, and unto Thyatira, and unto Sardis, and unto Philadelphia, and unto Laodicea.

God specifically told John to write the Revelation. From an island off the coast of modern day Turkey, John was given insight into 7 churches on the mainland.

12 And I turned to see the voice that spoke with me. And being turned, I saw seven golden candlesticks;

13 And in the midst of the seven candlesticks one like unto the Son of man, clothed with a garment down to the foot, and girt about the paps with a golden girdle.

14 His head and his hairs were white like wool, as white as snow; and his eyes were as a flame of fire;

15 And his feet like unto fine brass, as if they burned in a furnace; and his voice as the sound of many waters.

16 And he had in his right hand seven stars; and out of his mouth went a sharp two edged sword; and his countenance was as the sun shines in his strength.

17 And when I saw him, I fell at his feet as dead. And he laid his right hand upon me, saying unto me, Fear not; I am the first and the last;

18 I am he that lives, and was dead; and, behold, I am alive for evermore. Amen; and have the keys of hell and death.

There are many symbols in this book. Some of them will be revealed, and others will not. Little commentary will be provided for unexplained symbols.

19 Write the things which you have seen, and the things which are, and the things which shall be hereafter;

Many consider this to be an outline for the Revelation. "The things which you have seen" is either regarded as the past or the vision of Jesus above. "The things which are," refers to the present, which is defined to exist from John's time through today, the church age. "The things which shall be hereafter," is the future, defined as the time after the church age.

While I agree that John wrote about his vision of Jesus, I do not agree that a time referred to as the "present" can continue 2,000 years. In Rev 4:1, John is told, "I will show you things which must be hereafter." This is not a future event! Chapter 4 is a picture of heaven without Jesus. Jesus was absent from heaven only during the time he became a man on earth. Chapter 5 shows Jesus at the moment of his resurrection into heaven. While John will eventually report on events subsequent to his lifetime and even upon events subsequent to the church age; he will not rush into them.

John will write about his visions. In the visions, some things were current events for John, and some things were to be in the future from John's perspective. This is all verse 19 is conveying.

20 The mystery of the seven stars which you saw in my right hand, and the seven golden candlesticks. The seven stars are the angels of the seven churches; and the seven candlesticks which you saw are the seven churches.

Many of the symbols are explained. Appendix 1 contains a list of defined symbols.

7 stars = angels of the 7 churches
7 candlesticks = 7 churches

Chapter 2

In Chapters 2 and 3, John writes about his vision of Jesus, about events transpiring in his lifetime regarding 7 specific churches, and about eternal rewards which are specific to the church.

1 **Unto the angel of the church of Ephesus write; These things says he that holds the seven stars in his right hand, who walks in the midst of the seven golden candlesticks;**

Jesus holds the 7 angels, that is, he holds them accountable. Jesus also walks in the midst of the 7 churches. In Revelation 3:21, Jesus is seated on God's throne. We know that he is to remain there until his enemies become his footstool. Heb 10:12-13 "But this man, after he had offered one sacrifice for sins for ever, sat down on the right hand of God; From henceforth expecting till his enemies be made his footstool." Therefore, when Jesus is said to walk among the churches, he does so through the Holy Spirit who dwells inside Christians.

2 **I know your works, and your labor, and your patience, and how you can not bear them which are evil; and you have tried them which say they are apostles, and are not, and have found them liars;**
3 **And have borne, and have patience, and for my name's sake have labored, and have not fainted.**
4 **Nevertheless I have somewhat against you, because you have left your first love.**
5 **Remember therefore from where you have fallen, and repent, and do the first works; or else I will come unto you quickly, and will remove your candlestick out of his place, except you repent.**
6 **But this you have, that you hate the deeds of the Nicolaitanes, which I also hate.**

In the letters to the churches, events of John's day are listed. These are the events that "shortly came to pass" because "the time was at hand."

> **7** **He that has an ear, let him hear what the Spirit says unto the churches; To him that overcomes will I give to eat of the tree of life, which is in the midst of the paradise of God.**

John 8:47 "He that is of God hears God's words…" What the Holy Spirit is revealing to God's people is that the uniqueness of the individual churches during John's era will become common characteristics in churches throughout time. Rev 22:6 "…These sayings are faithful and true…" We can be confident that the prophecies of the Revelation are true because this prophecy about churches is true. It has been proven over and over for 2,000 years. Only the names have been changed.

In the events of Chapters 2 and 3, there is no escalation in intensity over time. For example, churches in our time exhibit the same patience they did during the 1st century. This is in contrast to the birth pang events of the first 5 seals of Chapter 6. For example, war has become more destructive over time.

Since church actions will not change over time, they are not signs of the return of Jesus. Since the first 5 seals will come with greater intensity over time, they are signs of the return of Jesus.

Christians have promises for a time after this life. These promises will again be seen in the last 2 chapters. They will be given to the whole church which will not be complete until the marriage of the Lamb. Rev 19:9 "…Blessed are they which are called unto the marriage supper of the Lamb…" Rev 21:7 sums up the promises. "He that overcomes will inherit all things; and I will be his God, and he shall be my son."

Since the purpose of this book is to reveal when the prophesied signs will take place in relation to one another, little commentary is provided about life in the church or life on the new earth once Jesus has renewed all things.

8 And unto the angel of the church in Smyrna write; These thing says the first and the last, which was dead, and is alive;

9 I know your works, and tribulation, and poverty, (but you are rich) and I know the blasphemy of them which say they are Jews, and are not, but are the synagogue of Satan.

10 Fear none of those things which you shall suffer; behold, the devil shall cast some of you into prison, that you may be tried; and you shall have tribulation ten days: be faithful unto death, and I will give you a crown of life.

11 He that has an ear, let him hear what the Spirit says unto the churches; He that overcomes shall not be hurt of the second death.

12 And to the angel of the church in Pergamos write; These things says he which has the sharp sword with two edges;

13 I know your works, and where you dwell, even where Satan's seat is: and you hold fast my name, and have not denied my faith, even in those days wherein Antipas was my faithful martyr, who was slain among you, where Satan dwells.

14 But I have a few things against you, because you have there them that hold the doctrine of Balaam, who taught Balak to cast a stumbling block before the children of Israel, to eat things sacrificed unto idols, and to commit fornication.

15 So have you also them that hold the doctrine of the Nicolaitanes, which thing I hate.

16 Repent; or else I will come unto you quickly, and will fight against them with the sword of my mouth.

17 He that has an ear, let him hear what the Spirit says unto the churches; To him that overcomes will I give to eat of the hidden manna, and will give him a white

stone, and in the stone a new name written, which no man knows saving he that receives it.

18 And unto the angel of the church in Thyatira write; These things says the Son of God, who has his eyes like unto a flame of fire, and his feet are like fine brass;

19 I know your works, and charity, and service, and faith, and your patience, and your works; and the last to be more than the first.

20 Notwithstanding I have a few things against you, because you suffer that woman Jezebel, which calls herself a prophetess, to teach and to seduce my servants to commit fornication, and to eat things sacrificed unto idols.

21 And I gave her space to repent of her fornication; and she repented not.

22 Behold, I will cast her into a bed, and them that commit adultery with her into great tribulation, except they repent of their deeds.

23 And I will kill her children with death; and all the churches shall know that I am he who searches the reins and hearts: and I will give unto every one of you according to your works.

24 But unto you I say, and unto the rest in Thyatira, as many as have not this doctrine, and which have not known the depths of Satan, as they speak; I will put upon you none other burden.

25 But that which you have already hold fast till I come.

26 And he that overcomes, and keeps my works unto the end, to him will I give power over the nations:

27 And he shall rule them with a rod of iron; as the vessels of a potter shall they be broken to shivers: even as I received of my Father.

28 And I will give him the morning star.

29 He that has an ear, let him hear what the Spirit says unto the churches.

Chapter 3

1 **And unto the angel of the church in Sardis write; These things says he that has the seven Spirits of God, and the seven stars; I know your works, that you have a name that you live, and are dead.**

2 **Be watchful, and strengthen the things which remain, that are ready to die: for I have not found your works perfect before God.**

3 **Remember therefore what you have received and heard, and hold fast, and repent. If therefore you shall not watch, I will come on you as a thief, and you shall not know what hour I will come upon you.**

Jesus said about his return in Mat 24:36 "But of that day and hour knows no man, no, not the angels of heaven, but my Father only." It is implied here that if we do watch for signs as his return draws closer, we will know about when Jesus will return, maybe even down to the very hour.

4 **You have a few names even in Sardis which have not defiled their garments; and they shall walk with me in white: for they are worthy.**

5 **He that overcomes, the same shall be clothed in white raiment; and I will not blot out his name out of the book of life, but I will confess his name before my Father, and before his angels.**

God is sovereign, but he also gives us choices. Once received, nothing can take away our salvation, but it appears we can give it back and be blotted out of the book of life.

6 **He that has an ear, let him hear what the Spirit says unto the churches.**

7 **And to the angel of the church in Philadelphia write; These things says he that is holy, he that is true, he that**

has the key of David, he that opens, and no man shuts; and shuts, and no man opens;

Chapter 15 of the Revelation describes a temple in heaven that opens and closes. Only those who belong to Jesus will be allowed in.

8   I know your works: behold, I have set before you an open door, and no man can shut it: for you have a little strength, and have kept my word, and have not denied my name.

9   Behold, I will make them of the synagogue of Satan, which say they are Jews, and are not, but do lie: behold, I will make them to come and worship before your feet, and to know that I have loved you.

10 Because you have kept the word of my patience, I also will keep you from the hour of temptation, which shall come upon all the world, to try them that dwell upon the earth.

This prophecy has found fulfillment from the first century. Christians will be kept from the hour of temptation through death. In the hour of temptation, the final hour of the great tribulation, Satan will appear as God when he kills God's 2 witnesses. Those accepting Jesus after this hour will be tried.

11 Behold, I come quickly: hold that fast which you have, that no man take your crown.

12 Him that overcomes will I make a pillar in the temple of my God, and he shall go no more out: and I will write upon him the name of my God, and the name of the city of my God, which is new Jerusalem, which comes down out of heaven from my God: and I will write upon him my new name.

Final fulfillment of this is pictured in Rev 20:4, "And I saw thrones, and they sat upon them, and judgment was given unto them…"

13 He that has an ear, let him hear what the Spirit says unto the churches.

14 And unto the angel of the church of the Laodiceans write; These things says the Amen, the faithful and true witness, the beginning of the creation of God;

15 I know your works, that you are neither cold nor hot: I would you were cold or hot.

16 So then because you are lukewarm, and neither cold nor hot, I will spew you out of my mouth.

17 Because you say, I am rich, and increased with goods, and have need of nothing; and know not you are wretched, and miserable, and poor, and blind, and naked:

18 I counsel you to buy of me gold tried in the fire, that you my be rich; and white raiment, that you may be clothed, and that the shame of your nakedness does not appear; and anoint your eyes with eye salve, that you may see.

19 As many as I love, I rebuke and chasten: be zealous therefore, and repent.

20 Behold, I stand at the door, and knock: if any man hear my voice, and open the door, I will come in to him, and will sup with him, and he with me.

21 To him that overcomes will I grant to sit with me in my throne, even as I also overcame, and am set down with my Father in his throne.

People will still repent of sin and accept the salvation of Jesus after the great tribulation. The people of this group, who die for their faith, successfully coming through the trial of verse 10 above, are pictured in the rest of Rev 20:4. "…and I saw the souls of them that were beheaded for the witness of Jesus, and for the word of God, and which had not worshipped the beast, neither had received his mark upon their foreheads, or in their hands; and they lived and reigned with Christ a thousand years."

22 He that has an ear, let him hear what the Spirit says unto the churches.

The vision for the churches was fulfilled during John's time, during our time, and it will continue to find fulfillment. Since the church is warned 7 times, we really should listen to God. He loves us and has made great promises to us!

Chapter 4

1 After this I looked, and, behold, a door was opened in heaven; and the first voice which I heard was as it were of a trumpet talking with me; which said, Come up hither, and I will show you things which must be hereafter.

"I will show you things which must be hereafter." This portion of the verse creates confusion. Many assume that the church is raptured or caught up into heaven at this point. For this to happen, bodies must first come out of their graves to be caught up into the air together with the living. 1 Thes 4:15. "For this we say unto you by the word of the Lord, that we which are alive and remain unto the coming of the Lord shall not prevent (arise before) them which are asleep (dead)." To this point in John's visions, the resurrection has not occurred. The first fruits of the first resurrection are seen in Chapter 14, and the remainder of the first resurrection comes to life in Chapter 20.

The term "hereafter" is used as it was in the 2nd chapter of Daniel. Dan 2:29 "As for you, O king, your thoughts came into your mind upon your bed, what should come to pass hereafter: and he that reveals secrets makes known to you what shall come to pass." Hereafter, according to the interpretation from God, began during the time of the king, more than 2,500 years ago. Dan 2:37 "You, O king, are a king of kings: for the God of heaven has given you a kingdom, power, and strength, and glory." Hereafter continued in the prophecy until the reign of Jesus. Dan 2:45 "Forasmuch as you saw that the stone was cut out of the mountain without hands, and that it broke in pieces the iron, the brass, the clay, the silver, and the gold; the great God has made known to the king what shall come to pass hereafter: and the dream is certain, and the interpretation thereof sure." In this scenario, hereafter begins at the time of the king and continues to the time of Jesus. Therefore, we can interpret the hereafter in verse 1 as meaning from now until any time in the future. Many people automatically interpret hereafter as meaning far into the future. In this verse, that is not the case.

> **2 And immediately I was in the spirit; and, behold, a throne was set in heaven, and one sat on the throne.**
> **3 And he that sat was to look upon like a jasper and a sardine stone; and there was a rainbow round about the throne, in sight like unto an emerald.**

From this description and the ones found in Chapters 21 and 22, it appears that the city of God is a crystal pyramid or prism. God himself is the source of pure light inside and the prism separates his light into the various colors of the rainbow.

> **4 And round about the throne were four and twenty seats: and upon the seats I saw four and twenty elders sitting, clothed in white raiment; and they had on their heads crowns of gold.**

Only one elder is mentioned in the Bible and his name is Melchisedec. Jesus became "...a priest for ever after the order of Melchisedec," as stated in Heb 7:17. Temple service was divided into 24 orders. The assigned order would serve during its course, half of a month.

Those who see the rapture of the church in verse 1, see the church symbolized by the 24 elders. This cannot be the case. The church is not resurrected until after Jesus' resurrection. At this point in the visions, He has not been resurrected. His resurrection does not occur until Rev 5:6. Therefore, the 24 seats with the 24 beings are the elders of the 24 orders, not the church itself. It would make sense that these beings will lead the church after its resurrection. They are not the church itself at any time.

> **5 And out of the throne proceeded lightnings and thunderings and voices: and there were seven lamps of fire burning before the throne, which are the seven Spirits of God.**

Defined Symbol: 7 lamps of fire before the throne = 7 Spirits of God

6   And before the throne there was a sea of glass like unto crystal: and in the midst of the throne, and round about the throne, were four beasts full of eyes before and behind.

7   And the first beast was like a lion, and the second beast like a calf, and the third beast had a face as a man, and the fourth beast was like a flying eagle.

8   And the four beasts had each of them six wings about him; and they were full of eyes within: and they rest not day and night, saying, Holy, holy, holy, Lord God Almighty, which was, and is, and is to come.

The 4 beasts are called cherubim in Ezekiel chapter 10. They appear to carry the throne of God. An interesting side note – there seems to be 2 seraphim missing in this passage from Revelation. In Isaiah 6:1-2, we recognize their existence "...I saw also the Lord sitting upon a throne, high and lifted up, and his train filled the temple. Above it stood the seraphims: each one had six wings; with two he covered his face, and with two he covered his feet, and with two he did fly." In Isaiah, we see the two seraphim and the four cherubim. Here in Revelation, the four cherubim are all that are mentioned, the seraphim have disappeared.

9   And when those beasts give glory and honor and thanks to him that sat on the throne, who lives for ever and ever,

10   The four and twenty elders fall down before him that sat on the throne, and worship him that lives for ever and ever, and cast their crowns before the throne, saying,

To cast a crown is to become humble.

11   You are worthy, O Lord, to receive glory and honor and power: for you created all things, and for your pleasure they are and were created.

There are many songs in heaven. This one refers to the creation, the one described in Genesis, not an event that will occur in the future.

Chapter 5

1   And I saw in the right hand of him that sat on the throne a book written within and on the backside, sealed with seven seals.
2   And I saw a strong angel proclaiming with a loud voice, Who is worthy to open the book, and to loose the seals thereof?
3   And no man in heaven, nor in earth, neither under the earth, was able to open the book, neither look thereon.

We already referenced the passage that stated no one could know the day or the hour of Jesus' return. That passage occurred before Jesus' resurrection. We will learn a lot more about the time of his return from the book in God's hand.

4   And I wept much, because no man was found worthy to open and to read the book, neither to look thereon.
5   And one of the elders said unto me, Weep not: behold, the Lion of the tribe of Judah, the Root of David, has prevailed to open the book, and to loose the seven seals thereof.
6   And I beheld, and lo, in the midst of the throne and of the four beasts, and in the midst of the elders, stood a Lamb as it had been slain, having seven horns and seven eyes, which are the seven Spirits of God sent forth into all the earth.

Contrary to the theory that Chapters 4-19 represent a time after the church age, in this Chapter 5 vision, Jesus is introduced into heaven, enabling the church age to begin.

This event is found in Hebrews 9:11-12 "But Christ being come an high priest of good things to come, by a greater and more perfect tabernacle, not made with hands, that is to say, not of this building; Neither by the blood of goats and calves, but by his own blood he entered in once into the holy place, having obtained eternal redemption for us."

In John 14:2-3, when Jesus said he was going to prepare a place for those who belong to him, I think this was the event he had in mind. The place was heaven. It already existed, but we could not enter. The souls of the dead could not enter heaven until the blood of Jesus was offered in the holy place. John 3:13 "And no man has ascended up to heaven, but he that came down from heaven, even the Son of man which is in heaven."

He is the king descended from the line of Judah, although he existed before David. He did not submit himself to Satan as did Adam and Eve. He paid the price for sin, he conquered death, and he will restore dominion over the earth to mankind. Taking his seat upon the throne, he sent his Holy Spirit to dwell within Christians.

Defined Symbol: 7 horns and 7 eyes of Jesus = 7 Spirits of God

7 **And he came and took the book out of the right hand of him that sat upon the throne.**
8 **And when he had taken the book, the four beasts and four and twenty elders fell down before the Lamb, having every one of them harps, and golden vials full of odors, which are the prayers of saints.**

Defined Symbol: odors in golden vials = prayers of saints

9 **And they sung a new song, saying, You are worthy to take the book, and to open the seals thereof: for you were slain, and have redeemed us to God by your blood out of every kindred, and tongue, and people, and nation;**
10 **And have made us unto our God kings and priests: and we shall reign on the earth.**

The 4 beasts and the 24 elders sing the prayers of the saints. This song is about the redemption of mankind through the sacrifice of Jesus. Just like Jesus, we will be made kings and priests. Some will be in the order of Melchisadec. The rest will be divided into the 23 other orders.

> **11 And I beheld, and I heard the voice of many angels round about the throne and the beasts and the elders: and the number of them was ten thousand times ten thousand, and thousands of thousands;**
>
> **12 Saying with a loud voice, Worthy is the Lamb that was slain to receive power, and riches, and wisdom, and strength, and honor, and glory, and blessing.**

There is rejoicing in heaven when anyone turns to Jesus, just as the shepherd rejoices when he finds his sheep that was lost. How much greater must have been this rejoicing over Jesus, who took upon himself all of our sins!

> **13 And every creature which is in heaven, and on the earth, and under the earth, and such as are in the sea, and all that are in them, heard I saying, Blessing, and honor, and glory, and power, be unto him that sits upon the throne, and unto the Lamb for ever and ever.**

One day, every creature from both heaven and earth will praise God.

John was told in Revelation 4:1 to come up into heaven to see the "hereafter." In contrast to the rest of the vision, this part is the only future event since that promise. The next purely future event will not take place until John opens the 6th seal.

> **14 And the four beasts said, Amen. And the four and twenty elders fell down and worshipped him that lives for ever and ever.**

Chapter 6

The 24th chapter of Matthew has many parallels with the Revelation. In Matt. 24:3, the disciples ask Jesus, "what will be the sign of your coming and of the end of the age? What is presumed in this question is that the return of Jesus will usher in a new age. Rev 20:4 states, "…They came to life and reigned with Christ a thousand years." Thus, the new age, the age to come after the church age, is commonly called the "millennium" or the "millennial reign of Christ." Jesus said in Matt 24:42, "keep awake therefore, for you do not know on what day your Lord is coming." Since we do not know the day in advance, signs of the Lord's coming are provided.

Seals 1-5 of this chapter are associated with "birth pangs" in Matt 24:5-9. John and the disciples experienced the sorrows found below. The difference between common occurrences in the church as listed in Chapters 2 and 3 and birth pangs; is that common experiences are not signs, while birth pangs are because they increase in intensity with shortened intervals between. Birth pangs will increase until the new age.

5   For many shall come in my name, saying, I am Christ; and shall deceive many.
6   And you shall hear of wars and rumors of wars: see that you are not troubled: for all these things must come to pass, but the end is not yet.
7   For nation shall rise against nation, and kingdom against kingdom: and there shall be famines, and pestilences, and earthquakes, in diverse places.
8   All these are the beginning of sorrows. (birth pangs)
9   Then shall they deliver you up to be afflicted, and shall kill you: and you shall be hated of all nations for my name's sake.

1   And I saw when the Lamb opened one of the seals, and I heard, as it were the noise of thunder, one of the four beasts saying, Come and see.

2   And I saw, and behold a white horse: and he that sat on him had a bow; and a crown was given unto him: and he went forth conquering, and to conquer.

Was Jesus the marker for the beginning of the end, or will the rise of antichrist be that marker?

By comparing Matt 24:5 with Rev 6:1-2, many commentators believe the antichrist is pictured in the 1st seal. I do not agree with this viewpoint. We will see in the 5th trumpet that the first appearance of the antichrist will come only after Satan is cast from heaven. At that time, death will be limited to 1/3 of the population. In these beginning birth pangs, death is limited to 1/4 of the population as revealed in the 4th seal.

This first seal fulfills Is 66:7. "Before she travailed, she brought forth; before her pain came, she was delivered of a man child." The birth pangs shown in seals 2-5 appear after the resurrection of Jesus. The birth pangs of our resurrection began when we received the Holy Spirit. Rom 8:22-23 "For we know that the whole creation groans and travails in pain together until now. And not only they, but ourselves also, which have the firstfruits of the Spirit, even we ourselves groan within ourselves, waiting for the adoption, to wit, the redemption of our body."

The first sign of our redemption was the resurrection of Jesus. The second sign is the seal of the Holy Spirit. Jesus conquered sin and death and continues to do so on our behalf through the Holy Spirit. This first seal pictures the formation of the kingdom of God. No limits are placed on this kingdom.

The bow is not a rainbow or a bow for arrows. In Strong's dictionary, it is the simplest fabric. This term is not used anywhere else in the Bible. As commonly used today, the bow is a symbol of hope.

3   And when he had opened the second seal, I heard the second beast say, Come and see.

4   And there went out another horse that was red: and power was given to him that sat thereon to take peace from the earth, and that they should kill one another: and there was given unto him a great sword.

This birth pang is war. Wars have increased in severity and they have come at closer intervals since the time of Jesus.

5   And when he had opened the third seal, I heard the third beast say, Come and see. And I beheld, and lo a black horse; and he that sat on him had a pair of balances in his hand.

6   And I heard a voice in the midst of the four beasts say, A measure of wheat for a penny, and three measures of barley for a penny; and see you hurt not the oil and the wine.

Famine is the next travail. In famine, a day of work only earns food for that day. Wheat and barley were the early or spring crops, while olives and grapes for oil and wine were not harvested until the fall. The conclusion to draw is that only famine from a failure of the early harvest is a sign of Jesus' return.

This seal also foreshadows future events. Rev 13:17 reveals that the limited number of remaining Christians will be unable to participate in the economy. Rev 16:21 will show the grape press of hail used by God used to squeeze blood (wine) from the plentiful number of wicked.

7   And when he had opened the fourth seal, I heard the voice of the fourth beast say, Come and see.

8   And I looked, and behold a pale horse: and his name that sat on him was Death, and Hell followed with him. And power was given unto them over the fourth part of the earth, to kill with the sword, and

with hunger, and with death, and with the beasts of the earth.

Pestilence is the sign of the pale horse. People will die and be buried, as a result of war, famine, and pestilence. Death is limited to 25% of the earth's population during the early birth pangs. The beasts of the earth are governments which have a hand in causing these problems. These are the nations and kingdoms of Matt 24:7 quoted earlier.

These plagues were foretold in regard to Jerusalem in Ezekiel 14:21. "For thus says the Lord God: How much more when I send my four sore judgments upon Jerusalem, the sword, and the famine, and the noisome beast, and the pestilence, to cut off from it man and beast?"

9   **And when he had opened the fifth seal, I saw under the altar the souls of them that were slain for the word of God, and for the testimony which they held:**

10   **And they cried with a loud voice, saying, How long, O Lord, holy and true, do you not judge and avenge our blood on them that dwell on the earth?**

11   **And white robes were given unto every one of them: and it was said unto them, that they should rest yet for a little season, until their fellow servants also and their brethren, that should be killed as they were, should be fulfilled.**

In contrast to the limited death of the 4th seal, there is no limit on Christian martyrdom. Their bodies have died, but their souls are with Jesus. Even in heaven, they don't have all the answers to what is coming on the earth. They have prayers of vengeance, which fill golden vials as found in Rev 5:8. Perhaps these are the vials which will be poured out in Chapter 16.

The first martyr of the New Testament was Stephen. Acts 7:59-60. "And they stoned Stephen, calling upon God, and saying, Lord Jesus receive my spirit. And he kneeled down, and cried with a loud voice, Lord, lay not this sin to their charge. And when he had said this, he fell asleep."

In verse 11 above, martyrs were given white robes, which is the righteousness of Jesus. Even though these martyrs are angrier than Stephen, this seal flows from the first seal where Jesus died and sent his Holy Spirit.

The last martyrs will be killed because they refuse to take the mark of the beast. Rev 20:4 "...and I saw the souls of them that were beheaded for the witness of Jesus, and for the word of God, and which had not worshipped the beast, neither his image, neither had received his mark upon their foreheads, or in their hands; and they lived and reigned with Christ a thousand years."

The 6th Seal

In order to understand the timing of the events of the Revelation, this seal must be understood. This seal exposes the signs surrounding the return of Jesus! This sequence of events is unchanging throughout John's visions. These events will be reviewed again and again through Chapter 19.

In the sequence of events found in the seals, this is the first one in which no part of John's vision was occurring during the time John wrote the book. As we've seen in Chapters 4, 5 and to this point in Chapter 6, when John was told he would see what was coming "hereafter," there was quite a build up for the "after" portion. Most of the rest of the Revelation will detail future events.

The great tribulation is one part of the end time events. The great tribulation is the lead in to the 6th seal.

For reference, the period of time known as the "great tribulation" will begin at the abomination of desolation. Matt 24:15-22.
> 15 When you therefore shall see the <u>abomination of desolation</u>, spoken of by Daniel the prophet, stand in the holy place, (whoso reads, let him understand:)
> 16 Then let them which be in Judaea flee into the mountains:
> 17 Let him which is on the housetop not come down to take any thing out of his house:
> 18 Neither let him which is in the field return back to take his clothes.
> 19 And woe unto them that are with child, and to them that give suck in those days!
> 20 But pray that your flight be not in the winter, neither on the Sabbath day:
> 21 For then shall be <u>great tribulation</u>, such as was not since the beginning of the world to this time, no, nor ever shall be.

22 And except those days should be shortened, there should no flesh be saved: but for the elect's sake those days shall be shortened.

When the time known as the "great tribulation" ends, the 6th seal will begin!

12 **And I beheld when he had opened the sixth seal, and, lo, there was a great earthquake; and the sun became black as sackcloth of hair, and the moon became as blood:**

13 **And the stars of heaven fell unto the earth, even as a fig tree cast her untimely figs, when she is shaken of a mighty wind.**

14 **And the heaven departed as a scroll when it is rolled together; and every mountain and island were moved out of their places.**

The order of events occurring within the 6th seal will take place as follows:

- the great earthquake which ends the great tribulation
- the sun, moon, star event
- the disappearance of physical heaven
- the appearance of spiritual heaven
- God's wrath

The great tribulation ends just prior to the sun, moon, star event. This is shown in Matthew 24:29, **"Immediately <u>after</u> the tribulation of those days** shall the sun be darkened, and the moon shall not give her light, and the stars shall fall from heaven, and the powers of the heavens shall be shaken:" The great tribulation does not last throughout the entire book of Revelation. It is only a portion of the pain and suffering that will be described. It has a definite beginning (the abomination of desolation) and a definite ending (the first great earthquake).

The ending of the great tribulation is the first event of the 6th seal (the first great earthquake).

Continuing with Matthew 24:29, we see the second event, which is the sun, moon, star event.

Matt 24:29 = Rev 6:12-13

"the sun be darkened" = "the sun became black as sackcloth of hair"
"the moon shall not give her light" = "the moon became as blood"
"the stars shall fall from heaven" = "the stars of heaven fell unto the earth"

Immediately after the first earthquake of this seal, the sun, moon, and stars will be darkened, and the sky will be rolled away (Rev 6:13 & 14a). The disappearance of the sky marks the 3rd event of the 6th seal.

When the sky rolls away, those of the earth will be able to see God and his dwelling place! This marks the 4th event of the 6th seal.

God's wrath is the 5th and final event of the 6th seal.

At this point in the Revelation, God's wrath is not clearly defined. However, it will be in Chapter 16. There, this wrath will be poured out in vials. Included in the vial judgments is a second great earthquake that will make all of the mountains and islands disappear. As shown below, the 6th seal and the 7th vial are the same; two descriptions of the same event.

6th seal – Rev 6:14 "every mountain and island were moved out of their places"
7th vial – Rev 16:20 "and every island fled away, and the mountains were not found"

This second earthquake will completely level the earth with the exception of Jerusalem.

15 And the kings of the earth, and the great men, and the rich men, and the chief captains, and the mighty men, and every bondman, and every free man, hid themselves in the dens and in the rocks of the mountains;

16 And said to the mountains and rocks, Fall on us, and hide us from the face of him that sits on the throne, and from the wrath of the Lamb:

17 For the great day of his wrath is come; and who shall be able to stand?

The climax of the period of time known as God's wrath is hail. After the 2nd great earthquake of Rev 16:20, the great day of God's wrath will come. A description of that day is found in Rev 16:21. "And there fell upon men a great hail out of heaven, every stone about the weight of a talent: and men blasphemed God because of the plague of the hail; for the plague thereof was exceedingly great."

The first six seals span the time from Jesus' resurrection until hail is ready to pour down upon those who will take the mark of the beast. The great tribulation and the 5 bulleted events of the 6th seal will be shown repeatedly through Chapter 19. Understanding this sequence is the greatest key to understanding the Revelation!

Chapter 7

1 And after these things I saw four angels standing on the four corners of the earth, holding the four winds of the earth, that the wind should not blow on the earth, nor on the sea, nor on any tree.

Daniel had a vision of 4 winds blowing, stirring up 4 great beasts. Dan 7:2-3 "...the four winds of the heaven strove upon the great sea. And four great beasts came up from the sea, diverse one from another." The beasts were symbols of kingdoms. Dan 7:23. "...The fourth beast shall be the fourth kingdom upon earth..."

The 4 kingdoms that ruled the world during a time when the Israeli people occupied their land were Babylon, Persia, Greece, and Rome. People occupying an area of these former kingdoms will once again be stirred up, and rule over Jerusalem.

2 And I saw another angel ascending from the east, having the seal of the living God: and he cried with a loud voice to the four angels, to whom it was given to hurt the earth and the sea,
3 Saying, Hurt not the earth, neither the sea, nor the trees, till we have sealed the servants of our God in their foreheads.

Christians have the seal of the living God. Eph 1:13 "In whom you also trusted, after you heard the word of truth, the gospel of your salvation: in whom also after you believed, you were sealed with that Holy Spirit of promise."

4 And I heard the number of them which were sealed: and there were sealed an hundred and forty and four thousand of all the tribes of the children of Israel.
5 Of the tribe of Judah were sealed twelve thousand. Of the tribe of Reuben were sealed twelve thousand. Of the tribe of Gad were sealed twelve thousand.

6   **Of the tribe of Asher were sealed twelve thousand. Of the tribe of Naphtali were sealed twelve thousand. Of the tribe of Manasseh were sealed twelve thousand.**

7   **Of the tribe of Simeon were sealed twelve thousand. Of the tribe of Levi were sealed twelve thousand. Of the tribe of Issachar were sealed twelve thousand.**

8   **Of the tribe of Zebulon were sealed twelve thousand. Of the tribe of Joseph were sealed twelve thousand. Of the tribe of Benjamin were sealed twelve thousand.**

God will choose 144,000 Israelites to become Christians. Messianic Jew is the popular term. These 144,000 Messianic Jews will become Christians before the four winds stir up another kingdom which will rule the world. In the midst of a 7 year treaty involving this world power, the abomination of desolation will be set up. Dan 9:27 "And he shall confirm the covenant with many for one week: and in the midst of the week he shall cause the sacrifice and the oblation to cease, and for the overspreading of abominations he shall make it desolate..." Although this portion of the Revelation is seen by John after the 6th seal, these Israelites will become Christians before the events of the 6th seal. Again, the order of events will be:

- 144,000 Jews will convert to Christianity
- The last Gentile world empire will arise
- There will be a 7 year covenant involving Israel
- The abomination of desolation will be set up, the start of great tribulation
- The great tribulation ends as the events of the 6th seal unfold

9   **After this I beheld, and, lo, a great multitude, which no man could number, of all nations, and kindreds, and people, and tongues, stood before the throne, and before the Lamb, clothed with white robes, and palms in the hands;**

10 **And cried with a loud voice, saying, Salvation to our God which sits upon the throne, and unto the Lamb.**

11 And all the angels stood round about the throne, and about the elders and the four beasts, and fell before the throne on their faces, and worshipped God,

12 Saying, Amen: Blessing, and glory, and wisdom, and thanksgiving, and honor, and power, and might, be unto our God for ever and ever. Amen.

13 And one of the elders answered, saying unto me, What are these which are arrayed in white robes: and whence came they?

14 And I said unto him, Sir, you know. And he said to me, These are they which came out of great tribulation, and have washed their robes, and made them white in the blood of the Lamb.

The martyrdom of the 5th seal will continue and increase as a birth pang, reaching vast numbers of people during the time of the great tribulation. However, martyrdom will not end there; it will continue even as God pours out his wrath.

Verse 14 shows that innumerable Christians will be slain during the period of great tribulation. From above, 4 events will take place before the events of the 6th seal. This Chapter only showed the conversion of the 144,000 and the great tribulation. The other events were mentioned to help clarify their timing.

15 Therefore are they before the throne of God, and serve him day and night in his temple: and he that sits on the throne shall dwell among them.

16 They shall hunger no more, neither thirst any more; neither shall the sun light on them, nor any heat.

17 For the Lamb which is in the midst of the throne shall feed them, and shall lead them unto living fountains of waters: and God shall wipe away all tears from their eyes.

Chapter 8

1 And when he had opened the seventh seal, there was silence in heaven about the space of half an hour.

After rejoicing in heaven in Rev 7:9-17, for all those who will go to heaven during the great tribulation, there will be silence in heaven for about 30 minutes while Christians get their Sabbath rest. The rest for the 144,000 will end when a voice from heaven says, "Come up hither." We will see that the 144,000 are the 2 witnesses of Chapter 11. This call from heaven will coincide with the great earthquake which begins the 6th seal and ends the great tribulation. This same earthquake will end the 2nd woe in Chapter 11. Rev 11:12-14.

12 And they heard a great voice from heaven saying unto them, Come up hither. And they ascended up to heaven in a cloud; and their enemies beheld them.

13 And the same hour was there a great earthquake, and the tenth part of the city fell, and in the earthquake was slain of men seven thousand: and the remnant were affrighted, and gave glory to the God of heaven.

14 The second woe is past; and, behold, the third woe comes quickly.

2 And I saw the seven angels which stood before God; and to them were given seven trumpets.

The 7 angels with 7 trumpets are separate from the seal sequence. They are not part of the 7th seal.

3 And another angel came and stood at the altar, having a golden censer; and there was given unto him much incense, that he should offer it with the prayers of all saints upon the golden altar which was before the throne.

At this point in the post tribulation sequence, physical heaven has been rolled away and spiritual heaven is visible. The heavenly golden altar is in the Holy of Holies with the Ark of the Covenant. The martyrs' prayers of vengeance will be answered. This follows the sequence of Rev 11:19. "And the temple of God was opened in heaven, and there was seen in his temple the ark of his testament: and there were lightings, and voices, and thunderings, and an earthquake, and great hail."

This earthquake of Rev 11:19, is also found in verse 5 below. This is the 2nd great earthquake found at the end of the 6th seal, and in Rev 16:18-21, the one that will cause the mountains and islands to be removed. After the earthquake, great hail will fall.

Rev 16:

18 And there were voices, and thunders, and lightnings; and there was a great earthquake, such as was not since men were upon the earth, so mighty an earthquake, and so great.

19 And the great city was divided into three parts, and the cities of the nations fell: and great Babylon came in remembrance before God, to give unto her the cup of the wine of the fierceness of his wrath.

20 And every island fled away, and the mountains were not found.

21 And there fell upon men a great hail out of heaven...

4   And the smoke of the incense, which came with the prayers of the saints, ascended up before God out of the angel's hand.

5   And the angel took the censer, and filled it with fire of the altar, and cast it into the earth: and there were voices, and thunderings, and lightnings, and an earthquake.

The sequence of the 6th seal was followed:
After the great tribulation, there will be silence in spiritual heaven.
Spiritual heaven will become visible.
God's wrath will be poured out, which includes the 2nd great earthquake.

This ends the 7th seal. The important parts of the 7th seal are that God will give everyone a Sabbath, a time of rest in heaven as promised in Heb 4:1-10; and that judgment from God will come upon the earth as a result of prayer. The voices, thunderings, and lightnings, were repeated to show that the earthquake of Rev 8:5 is the 2nd great earthquake, the one that levels the earth.

The seal sequence has ended. It began with the resurrection of Jesus, continued through the return of Jesus, and finished when his wrath was poured out. The trumpet sequence will now begin.

6 And the seven angels which had the seven trumpets prepared themselves to sound.

The angels with trumpets represent a new section of the Revelation. The signs of the trumpets do not repeat like the signs of the first five seals. The trumpets will picture specific signs or one time events that will more clearly signal the return of Jesus.

The seal signs began at the time of Jesus. The trumpet signs may have started at World War II or they may start with a future great war. In either case, the time frame for the trumpets is much shorter than it is for the seals. There is no time frame provided for trumpets 1-6, except that they will occur before the start of the great tribulation. The 6th trumpet will blow about the time of the covenant of Dan 9:27 quoted earlier. The 7th trumpet will include the return of Jesus which will come after the great tribulation, after the physical heaven has been rolled away, and after the spiritual heaven has been revealed.

The birth pang signs of death from war, famine, pestilence, and kingdoms; will still exist during the times of the trumpets, but they will no longer be limited to 25% of earth's population. The 1st and 5th seals representing Christianity and martyrdom will also continue. Both the seal and trumpet sequences end with hail on the great day of the wrath of God.

7   The first angel sounded, and there followed hail and fire mingled with blood, and they were cast upon the earth: and the third part of trees was burnt up, and all green grass was burnt up.

This trumpet appears to signal a world war.

8   And the second angel sounded, and as it were a great mountain burning with fire was cast into the sea: and the third part of the sea became blood;
9   And the third part of the creatures which were in the sea, and had life, died; and the third part of the ships were destroyed.

The sea can be symbolic of the nations, especially the nations around the Mediterranean Sea.

The great mountain pictures a great city that will be destroyed.
Jer. 51:24-25
24   And I will render unto Babylon and to all the inhabitants of Chaldea all their evil that they have done in Zion in your sight, says the Lord.
25   Behold, I am against you, O destroying mountain, says the Lord, which destroys all the earth: and I will stretch out my hand upon you, and roll you down from the rocks, and will make you a burnt mountain.

Today, the great city is not Babylon. The city responsible for bringing evil upon the people of Israel will be the city that brings this specific judgment upon itself.

10   And the third angel sounded, and there fell a great star from heaven, burning as it were a lamp, and it fell upon the third part of the rivers, and upon the fountains of waters;
11   And the name of the star is called Wormwood: and the third part of the waters became wormwood; and many men died of the waters, because they were made bitter.

The Ukrainian word for Wormwood is Chernobyl. This is significant because this is the place of a great nuclear accident. Radiation killed so many that the name Chernobyl is forever linked to radiation. This also links Wormwood to radiation. If Chernobyl fulfilled the 3rd trumpet, then the 1st trumpet was World War II, and the great city that was destroyed in the 2nd trumpet was Berlin. It should also be noted that the nation of Israel came back into existence as a result of the holocaust and of the 2nd World War.

12 And the fourth angel sounded, and the third part of the sun was smitten, and the third part of the moon, and the third part of the stars; so as the third part of them was darkened, and the day shone not for a third part of it, and the night likewise.

A mushroom cloud appears after a nuclear blast, blocking the view of the sky and raining radiation into the rivers. The sky is prophesied to be dark from the cloud for 8 hours, 4 hours before sunset, until 4 hours after sunset. Since the Chernobyl blast occurred in the wee hours of the morning, there is not a certainty that these 4 trumpets have been blown. However, the names of Wormwood and Chernobyl in this context can not be ignored!

Even if the Chernobyl explosion was not the fulfillment of the 3rd and 4th trumpets, this would not negate World War II and Berlin as possible fulfillments of trumpets 1 and 2.

13 And I beheld, and heard an angel flying through the midst of heaven, saying with a loud voice, Woe, woe, woe, to the inhabitants of the earth by reason of the other voices of the trumpet of the three angels, which are yet to sound!

Some of the events of Chapters 8 and 9 of the Revelation are parallel to events in Chapter 12.

World war on earth will be associated with heavenly war.
8:7 The first angel sounded, and there followed hail and fire mingled with blood, and they were cast upon the earth: and the

third part of trees was burnt up, and all green grass was burnt up.
12:7 And there was war in heaven: Michael and his angels fought against the dragon; and the dragon fought and his angels.

The aggressors of earth and heaven will be defeated.
8:8 And the second angel sounded, and as it were a great mountain burning with fire was cast into the sea: and the third part of the sea became blood.
12:8 And prevailed not; neither was their place found any more in heaven.

The fall of the Wormwood star is comparable to the fall of Satan.
8:10 And the third angel sounded, and there fell a great star from heaven…
12:9 And the great dragon was cast out, that old serpent, called the Devil, and Satan…

The darkness of the sky pictures the casting out of the defeated angels.
8:12 And the fourth angel sounded, and the third part of the sun was smitten, and the third part of the moon, and the third part of the stars; so as the third part of them was darkened, and the day shone not for a third part of it, and the night likewise.
12:9 …and his (Satan's) angels were cast out with him.

Woe comes to the earth when Satan is cast out of heaven.
8:13 …woe, woe, woe, to the inhabiters of the earth by reason of the other voices of the trumpet of the three angels…
12:12 "…Woe to the inhabitants of the earth and of the sea! For the devil is come down to you, having great wrath, because he knows he has but a short time."

The parallels continue in Chapter 9 with satanic attacks against Israel.

Satan will persecute Israel using the locust army of the 5th trumpet (Rev 9:1-12) and the 200,000,000 cavalry of the 6th trumpet (Rev 9:13-21).

12:13 "And when the dragon saw that he was cast unto the earth, he persecuted the woman which brought forth the man child."

Without these parallel sections, we would not necessarily know that the statement found in Rev 12:13 is a direct reference to the 5th and 6th trumpets! The failure of Satan's armies to exterminate Israel in trumpets 5 and 6 leads to the end of Chapter 12 where Satan sets out to exterminate Christians using the final gentile world empire of Chapter 13.

Just as understanding the 6th seal is the key to understanding the timing of the Revelation, understanding the above parallels is necessary for understanding how spiritual warfare will affect the earth in the end times!

Chapter 9

1 **And the fifth angel sounded, and I saw a star fall from heaven unto the earth: and to him was given the key of the bottomless pit.**

This star is the same one that fell in the 3rd trumpet. In addition to being a nuclear blast, it is also a picture of Satan being cast to earth, bringing about the 1st woe. In giving Satan the key to the bottomless pit, Satan will acquire the authority to release angels who have been bound there. It will be like a scene from the movie "Ghost Busters."

Jude 6 talks about angels who have been chained in the pit. "And the angels which kept not their first estate, but left their own habitation, he has reserved in everlasting chains under darkness unto the judgment of the great day."

In Chapter 20, the angel Satan will be bound.
1   And I saw an angel come down from heaven, having the key of the bottomless pit and a great chain in his hand.
2   And he laid hold on the dragon, that old serpent, which is the Devil, and Satan, and bound him a thousand years.

2 **And he opened the bottomless pit; and there arose a smoke out of the pit, as the smoke of a great furnace; and the sun and the air were darkened by reason of the smoke of the pit.**

The bottomless pit or hell is also the place for the spirits of the dead. This place can never be filled. When Jesus rose from the dead, he took the spirits of those who belong to him from the pit up into heaven with him. Prior to His resurrection, the place for the spirits of the dead included both the good and the evil spirits. When Jesus took the good with him, he ended the time of the good waiting in hell for ascension. Eph 4:8 "…When he ascended up on high, he led captivity captive, and gave (spiritual) gifts unto men."

There is no longer a place in the earth for the spirits of those who belong to Jesus. Again, in the rich man and Lazarus story, we see the gulf or separation between the 2 sides of this bottomless pit. (Luke 16:19-31) But when Jesus took the good with him as he ascended, he showed us that to die is to be with the Lord, as it says in 2 Cor 5:8 "...to be absent from the body, and to be present with the Lord."

The darkened air is likely a restatement of the 4th trumpet.

> **3 And there came out of the smoke locusts upon the earth: and unto them was given power, as the scorpions of the earth have power.**

No army was sent forth as a result of the Chernobyl explosion. This fact casts much doubt on that explosion as a fulfillment of the 3rd trumpet.

> **4 And it was commanded them that they should not hurt the grass of the earth, neither any green thing, neither any tree; but only those men which have not the seal of God in their foreheads.**
> **5 And to them it was given that they should not kill them, but that they should be tormented five months: and their torment was as the torment of a scorpion, when he strikes a man.**
> **6 And in those days shall men seek death, and shall not find it; and shall desire to die, and death shall flee from them.**

As seen in the parallel account at the end of Chapter 8, Satan's initial persecution will be directed toward Israel. The 144,000 Messianic Jews will not be harmed even if they are on the scene at this point. Some form of non-lethal chemical or biological weapon will be released that will be harmful to man, but not to plants.

The 11th chapter of Daniel beginning with verse 13 describes war that will be waged against Israel by kings to the north of Israel shortly before Jesus returns. Trumpets 3 and 4 will likely be fulfilled when a city to the north of Israel is hit with a nuclear bomb. The locust army will likely be a counter offensive ordered by a leader from the north who will survive the explosion.

It is not hard to imagine a current scenario for fulfillment of trumpets 3-5: Damascus, Syria, gets hit with a nuclear bomb. Nuclear fallout ensues. The Syrian leader survives and goes on the offensive, firing chemical weapons upon its neighbors for 5 months.

> 7 **And the shapes of the locusts were like unto horses prepared unto battle; and on their heads were as it were crowns like gold, and their faces were as the faces of men.**
> 8 **And they had hair as the hair of women, and their teeth were as the teeth of lions.**
> 9 **And they had breastplates, as it were breastplates of iron; and the sound of their wings was as the sound of chariots or many horses running to battle.**

From this description, the locusts involved in the counter attack are most likely helicopters. John used 1st century language to describe modern day warfare.

> 10 **And they had tails like unto scorpions, and there were stings in their tails: and their power was to hurt men five months.**
> 11 **And they had a king over them, which is the angel of the bottomless pit, whose name in the Hebrew tongue is Abaddon, but in the Greek tongue his name is Apollyon.**

Abaddon and Apollyon mean destroyer. The destroyer was the entity that killed the first born in the 10th and final plague of the Exodus. One theory explains the destroyer as poison gas, and that fits the description of what will happen here. Although the gas will not be fatal, it will cause great pain.

The first of Satan's armies after he is cast from heaven will come to its end after 5 months. The 5 month northern leader will become the antichrist.

The destroyer was there for the first Passover. It is interesting that Orthodox Jews look for Elijah during their annual remembrance of Passover. Perhaps at a Passover meal during this trumpet, the 144,000 Messianic Jews will explain to Israel that Jesus is the Passover Lamb, and cause repentance. More will be said about Elijah in Rev 11:5-6.

12 **One woe is past; and, behold, there come two woes more hereafter.**
13 **And the sixth angel sounded, and I heard a voice from the four horns of the golden altar which is before God,**
14 **Saying to the sixth angel which had the trumpet, Loose the four angels which are bound in the great river Euphrates.**

Once again, angels that were once bound will be set free. The call to "Loose the four angels" may be the shout, the first of three sounds signaling the return of Jesus. 1 Thes 4:16 "For the Lord himself shall descend from heaven with a shout..." This shout is a command or incitement, and it fits the context.

15 **And the four angels were loosed, which were prepared for an hour, and a day, and a month, and a year, for to slay the third part of men.**
16 **And the number of the army of the horsemen were two hundred thousand thousand: and I heard the number of them.**
17 **And thus I saw the horses in the vision, and them that sat on them, having breastplates of fire, and of jacinth, and brimstone: and the heads of the horses were as the heads of lions; and out of their mouths issued fire and smoke and brimstone.**
18 **By these three was the third part of men killed, by the fire, and by the smoke, and by the brimstone, which issued out of their mouths.**

19 For their power is in their mouth, and in their tails: for their tails were like unto serpents, and had heads, and with them they do hurt.

Just as each church had an angel who was responsible for it in Chapters 2 and 3 ("to the angel of the church of ..."); the 4 angels of this section will have influence upon 4 nations along the Euphrates River. These angels will spur their 4 nations to begin the second attack against Israel. The Euphrates River flows through Turkey, Syria, and Iraq. It also borders Iran as it flows into the Persian Gulf. These 4 nations will likely be the source of the 2 million cavalry.

Israel was attacked in 1948; the day after foreign powers granted it sovereignty. The same may occur when Israel resumes animal sacrifice in Jerusalem as it returns to God's covenant. Here again, the way Israel will return to this covenant is when a stronger power grants Israel the authority to do so. The granting of this authority to Israel may bring about the next invasion. This invasion may be the second day of the last 7 years of Gentile rule over Israel as prophesied in Dan 9:27. "And he shall confirm the covenant with many for one week: and in the midst of the week he shall cause the sacrifice and the oblation to cease, and for the overspreading of abominations he shall make it desolate, even until the consummation, and that determined shall be poured upon the desolate." This would contradict the peaceful start to the final 7 years that many predict.

Many of the prophecies of Daniel can be woven into the Revelation at the point where Satan is cast to the earth; first persecuting Israel, then Christians. I will attempt to do a little of this here and in the next chapter. Understanding the book of Daniel is necessary for understanding the Revelation.

An account of this 4 angel invasion is found in Dan 11:13-19 and repeated in Dan 11:40-45. In these accounts, Greece was the third empire prophesied by Daniel to rule the world. Out of this empire 4 lesser leaders were foretold. Of the four, 2 were important in Israel's history. The king of the north represents Seleucia, a

General from the army of Alexander the Great, who took control of the area to the north of Israel. The king of the south represents Ptolemy, a Greek General who took charge over the area to the south of Israel. These 2 lesser empires spent years fighting each other and ruling Israel.

When Satan unlocks the angel from the pit, this angel will influence a government figure to act as someone who has died. In this case, Seleucia will be the kingdom that will come out of the bottomless pit, and it will take 3 different forms. The first form will last for 5 months. It was described in the 5th trumpet. The second form of the Seleucian Empire will be the confederation of 4 nations found in the 6th trumpet. The last form will resemble the first who had power for 5 months. It may even have the same leader. This last form of Seleucia will gain power over the last Gentile world empire. This Gentile Empire or New Roman Empire is described in Chapter 13.

An example of someone in the present acting as a past leader occurred during the reign of Saddam Hussein of Iraq. He rebuilt the walls of Babylon as they were under King Nebuchadnezzar more than 2,500 years ago. Satan may have freed an angel from the pit, who then influenced King Hussein to act as he did. This is not a biblical sign of Jesus return, just an observation. The rebuilding of Seleucia will foreshadow the antichrist.

Following is the Daniel account of the 6th trumpet.

Daniel 11

13 For the king of the north shall return, and shall set forth a multitude greater than the former, and shall certainly come after certain years with a great army and with much riches.
14 And in those times there shall many stand up against the king of the south: also the robbers of thy people shall exalt themselves to establish the vision: but they shall fail.

15 So the king of the north shall come, and cast up a mount, and take the most fenced cities; and the arms of the south shall not withstand, neither his chosen people, neither shall there be any strength to withstand.

16 But he that comes against him shall do according to his own will, and none shall stand before him: and he shall stand in the glorious land, which by his hand shall be consumed.

17 He shall also set his face to enter with the strength of his whole kingdom, and upright ones with him; thus shall he do: and he shall give him the daughter of women, corrupting her: but she shall not stand on his side, neither be for him.

18 After this shall he turn his face unto the isles, and shall take many: but a prince for his own behalf shall cause the reproach offered by him to cease; without his own reproach he shall cause it to turn upon him.

19 Then he shall turn his face toward the fort of his own land: but he shall stumble and fall, and not be found.

Repetition of the same account

40 And at the time of the end shall the king of the south push at him; and the king of the north shall come against him like a whirlwind, with chariots, and with horsemen, and with many ships; and he shall enter into the countries, and shall overflow and pass over.

41 He shall enter also into the glorious land, and many countries shall be overthrown: but these shall escape out of his hand, even Edom, and Moab, and the chief of the children of Ammon.

42 He shall stretch forth his hand also upon the countries: and the land of Egypt shall not escape.

43 But he shall have power over the treasures of gold and of silver, and over all the precious things of

Egypt: and the Libyans and the Ethiopians shall be at his steps.

44 But tidings out of the east and out of the north shall trouble him: therefore he shall go forth with great fury to destroy and utterly to make away many.

45 And he shall plant the tabernacles of his palace between the seas in the glorious holy mountain; yet he shall come to his end, and none shall help him.

Another account of this gathering is found in Ezekiel, chapter 38.

20 And the rest of the men which were not killed by these plagues yet repented not of the works of their hands, that they should not worship devils, and idols of gold, and silver, and brass, and stone, and of wood: which neither can see, nor hear, nor walk:

21 Neither did they repent of their murders, nor of their sorceries, nor of their fornication, nor of their thefts.

Neither the people of Israel, nor the people who attacked them will repent of their deeds.

Chapter 10

1   And I saw another mighty angel come down from heaven, clothed with a cloud: and a rainbow was upon his head, and his face was as it were the sun, and his feet as pillars of fire:

This is a picture of the archangel Michael. He will give John inside information on what else will be taking place during the latter time of the trumpet progression.

After defeating Satan in heaven, Michael will come to the earth to protect Israel during the time of woe. Rev 12:7 "And there was war in heaven: Michael and his angels fought against the dragon; and the dragon fought and his angels." Dan 12:1 "And at that time, shall Michael stand up, the great prince which stands for the children of your people: and there shall be a time of trouble, such as never was since there was a nation even to that same time: and at that time your people shall be delivered, every one that shall be found written in the book." The time of trouble will be the great tribulation which will begin with the abomination of desolation and end with the first great earthquake.

2   And he had in his hand a little book open: and he set his right foot upon the sea, and his left foot on the earth,

Jesus was able to open the 7 seals of a book, so that might be the open book. More likely, this is the book of Daniel which is now open.

3   And cried with a loud voice, as when a lion roars: and when he had cried, seven thunders uttered their voices.

This sound is likely the voice of the archangel in 1:Thes 4:16 "For the Lord himself shall descend from heaven with a shout, with the voice of the archangel..." As previously noted, the shout was likely Rev 9:14 "...Loose the four angels which are bound in the great river Euphrates." This will be followed by the voice of the archangel mentioned here.

4   And when the seven thunders had uttered their voices, I was about to write: and I heard a voice from heaven saying unto me, Seal up those things which the seven thunders uttered, and write them not.

Seven seals, 7 trumpets, and later, 7 vials or bowls will be revealed. In contrast, these 7 thunders are not revealed. Daniel's book, although it can now be understood, was to be sealed until the time of the end. Dan 12:4. "But you, O Daniel, shut up the words, and seal the book, even to the time of the end…"

Since everything else John sees is revealed for the churches, the thunders may instead have a message for Israel.

5   And the angel which I saw stand upon the sea and upon the earth lifted up his hand to heaven,
6   And swore by him that lives for ever and ever, who created heaven, and the things that are therein, and the sea, and the things which are in them, that there should be time no longer:
7   But in the days of the voice of the seventh angel, when he shall begin to sound, the mystery of God should be finished, as he has declared to his servants the prophets.

The mystery of God is revealed in Rev 11:15. "…The kingdoms of this world are become the kingdoms of our Lord, and of his Christ; and he shall reign for ever and ever."

The mention of the prophets in verse 7 gives further evidence that the scroll in Jesus' hand was the word that was given to the prophet Daniel.

8   And the voice which I heard from heaven spoke unto me again, and said, Go and take the little book which is open in the hand of the angel which stands upon the sea and upon the earth.

9 And I went unto the angel, and said unto him, Give me the little book. And he said unto me, Take it, and eat it up; and it shall make your belly bitter, but it shall be in your mouth sweet as honey.

10 And I took the little book out of the angel's hand, and ate it up; and it was in my mouth sweet as honey: and as soon as I had eaten it, my belly was bitter.

It is great to gain understanding of God's word, but the revealed destruction can make your stomach turn.

11 And he said unto me, You must prophesy again before many peoples, and nations, and tongues, and kings.

Rather than pushing further into the future from the time of the 6th trumpet, it is time to go back and provide background into other things that will occur around this time. Background can be found in the 7 prophetic chapters of the book of Daniel.

Daniel

In chapter 2, king Nebuchadnezzar had a dream about the gentile kingdoms of the earth that would reign over the whole world. Daniel revealed that Babylon was the first of the 4. The second was Medo-Persia, the third was Greece, and the fourth was Rome. There will be a future part of the 4th kingdom, which will consist of 10 united governments. When the future Roman Empire with 10 leaders exists, Jesus will come.

In chapter 7, the same 4 kingdoms are revealed. During the future part of the Roman Empire, a small kingdom will also arise. The small kingdom will gain control over the future Roman Empire. The future Roman Empire will come to its end when Jesus returns.

Chapter 8 reveals that the Grecian Empire was to be broken into 4 parts. The northern part was known as the Seleucian Empire. There will be a future Seleucian Empire from which the antichrist will come. Antichrist will be removed when Jesus rules.

In chapter 9 we learn specifically about 490 years of Gentile rule over the land and people of Israel. A holy covenant will be confirmed which will begin the last 7 years of Gentile rule over Israel. At the start of this covenant, sacrifice and offerings will be offered to God by Israel as they were in Old Testament times. However this sacrifice will be stopped in the midst of the 7 years.

Chapter 10 describes the spiritual forces behind the world governments. The prince of the kingdom of Persia was the spiritual force behind the Medo-Persian Empire. The spiritual force of Greece was prophesied to rise after the prince of Persia. The archangel Michael is revealed as the prince or spiritual leader of Israel.

Chapter 11 prophesies a great king from Greece defeating a Persian king. The Grecian Empire was to be split into 4 lesser parts. In the beginning, these kingdoms were led by Alexander's Generals. The kingdom to the north of Israel was led by Seleucia. The kingdom to the south of Israel was led by Ptolemy. Over the years, these 2 kingdoms fought against one another. These 2 old enemies will resume their fight near the time of the return of Jesus. The future Seleucian Empire is represented in the 5th and 6th trumpets of the Revelation. When the invasion force of the 6th trumpet is slaughtered, the 5 month king of the 5th trumpet will return. He will be the antichrist who will take over the future version of the Roman Empire.

The 12th chapter reveals that at the time of the abomination of desolation, the Archangel Michael will fight for Israel. This will be the period known as the great tribulation. The great tribulation will last for 1,260 days, ending with the death and resurrection of Jesus' 2 witnesses. Antichrist will not be removed for another 30 days. This will be day 1,290 after the abomination of desolation. The great hail, the last plague in the period of God's wrath will not end until day 1,335.

Some version of the previous 7 paragraphs is likely what the 7 thunders had to say, as these paragraphs provide background for this portion of the Revelation. If this interpretation of Daniel is correct, it is the time of the end. These prophecies were to be sealed or unknown until the time of their fulfillment.

Chapter 11

This chapter begins at the time the 6th trumpet is blown. These events will pertain to the last 7 years of Gentile rule on earth. The 7 years will end when the 7th trumpet is blown. However, this chapter continues past the 7th trumpet, ending with hail, the judgment of the great day of God's wrath.

1 And there was given me a reed like unto a rod: and the angel stood, saying, Rise, and measure the temple of God, and the altar, and them that worship therein.

There will be a Jewish Temple built on its former location in Jerusalem. The system of animal sacrifice will resume at the start of the rebuilding of the Temple.

2 But the court which is without the temple leave out, and measure it not; for it is given unto the Gentiles: and the holy city shall they tread under foot forty and two months.

Dan 9:27 which has already been quoted reveals that Gentile authorities will recognize the covenant between God and Israel that requires animal sacrifice. For the first 42 months of the 7 years, Jews will worship on the Temple Mount in Jerusalem right along side of Gentiles. Islam's Dome of the Rock is currently on the Temple Mount and it will likely remain there during fulfillment of this prophecy.

For a fuller understanding of this time, read Dan 11:13-45. The 4 kingdom federation of the 6th trumpet is the king of the north listed in verses 13-19 and again in verses 40-45. Antichrist, the deposed 5 month leader of the 5th trumpet is the king of the north who returns to power in verse 21. "And in his estate shall stand up a vile person to whom they shall not give the honor of the kingdom: but he shall come in peaceably, and obtain the kingdom by flatteries." Antichrist's confederation with the 10 king, new Roman

Empire begins in verse 23. "And after the league made with him he shall work deceitfully: for he shall come up, and shall become strong with a small people." The abomination of desolation is listed in verse 31. "And arms shall stand on his part, and they shall pollute the sanctuary of strength, and shall take away the daily sacrifice, and they shall place the abomination that makes desolate." Thirty days later, antichrist will take over the new Roman Empire and reign for 42 months.

There has been a time in Israel's history found in 1 Maccabees that foreshadows the prophecies of this chapter. A Seleucian ruler named Antiochus Epiphanes acted as antichrist. In 1 Mac 1:54 his armies "erected a desolating sacrilege on the altar of burnt offering" on the 15th day of Chislev. Verse 59 states "On the twenty-fifth day of the month they offered sacrifice on the altar that was on top of the altar of burnt offering."

The abomination of desolation in the days of Antiochus Epiphanes was an altar built on top of the altar that Israel was using for animal sacrifice. It will likely be the same in the future.

3   And I will give power unto my two witnesses, and they shall prophesy a thousand and threescore days, clothed in sackcloth.

The second half of the 7 years, the next 42 months will start with the abomination of desolation. The armies of antichrist will cause covenant sacrifice to cease.

At that time, Israelites who know the prophecies of Daniel will be led by these 2 witnesses into the wilderness. They will flee from Jerusalem into the desert. These 1,260 days, roughly 3.5 years, will become the days known as the great tribulation. An account of this time is given in Matt 24:15-28. Verses 15-22 were quoted in Chapter 6. Following are verses 23-28.

23 Then if any man shall say unto you, Lo, here is Christ, or there; believe it not.

24 For there shall arise false Christs, and false prophets, and shall show great signs and wonders; insomuch that, if it were possible, they shall deceive the very elect.

25 Behold, I have told you before.

26 Wherefore if they shall say unto you, Behold, he is in the desert; go not forth: behold, he is in the secret chambers; believe it not.

27 For as the lightning comes out of the east, and shines even unto the west; so shall also the coming of the Son of man be.

28 For wheresoever the carcass is, there will the eagles be gathered together.

4 These are the two olive trees, and the two candlesticks standing before the God of the earth.

God called the nation of Israel an olive tree. Not long after Israel became a kingdom, it split into the northern kingdom named Israel and the southern kingdom named Judah. The 2 olive trees are symbols for the northern and southern sections of the nation of Israel.

Jeremiah 11:16-17

16 The Lord called thy name, A green olive tree, fair, and of goodly fruit: with the noise of a great tumult he has kindled fire upon it, and the branches of it are broken.

17 For the Lord of hosts, that planted you, has pronounced evil against you, for the evil of the house of Israel and of the house of Judah, which they have done against themselves to provoke me to anger in offering incense unto Baal.

We learned in Rev 1:20 that candlesticks represent churches. Here, the 2 candlesticks symbolize the church of Israel and the church of Judah. The 2 witnesses are not 2 individuals, but 2 churches comprised of the 144,000 Messianic Jews introduced in Chapter 7.

5   And if any man will hurt them, fire proceeds out of their mouth, and devours their enemies: and if any man will hurt them, he must in this manner be killed.

The prophet Elijah called fire down from heaven to destroy his enemies. 2 Kings 1:10 "And Elijah answered and said to the captain of fifty, If I be a man of God, then let fire come down from heaven, and consume you and your fifty. And there came down fire from heaven, and consumed him and his fifty." The 144,000 will have the power of Elijah to fight against their enemies.

6   These have power to shut heaven, that it rain not in the days of their prophecy: and have power over waters to turn them to blood, and to smite the earth with all plagues, as often as they will.

Elijah also prayed and caused the rain to cease for 3.5 years.

In Matt 11:12-14, Jesus said that John the Baptist was Elijah because both had the same spirit and power. The 144,000 will also be given the spirit and power of Elijah for 1,260 days just prior to Jesus' return. Both John the Baptist and the 144,000 fulfill Mal 4:5, "Behold, I will send you Elijah the prophet before the coming of the great and dreadful day of the Lord."

7   And when they shall have finished their testimony, the beast that ascends out of the bottomless pit shall make war against them, and shall overcome them, and kill them.

As mentioned in the commentary of verse 2, the king of the north from the 5th trumpet will return. He will come back as from the dead. This will be the antichrist and he will kill the 144,000 Messianic Jews. This is the one foretold in 2 Thes 2:3-12.

> 3   Let no man deceive you by any means: for that day shall not come, except there come a falling away first, and that man of sin be revealed, the son of perdition;

4   Who opposes and exalts himself above all that is called God, or that is worshipped; so that he as God sits in the temple of God, showing himself that he is God.

5   Don't you remember that when I was yet with you, I told you these things?

6   And now you know what withholds that he might be revealed in his time.

7   For the mystery of iniquity does already work: only he who now lets will let, until he be taken out of the way.

8   And then shall that Wicked be revealed, whom the Lord shall consume with the spirit of his mouth, and shall destroy with the brightness of his coming:

9   Even him, whose coming is after the working of Satan with all power and signs and lying wonders,

10 And with all deceivableness of unrighteousness in them that perish; because they received not the love of the truth, that they might be saved.

11 And for this cause God shall send them strong delusion, that they should believe a lie.

12 That they all might be damned who believed not the truth, but had pleasure in unrighteousness.

The Archangel Michael is shown fighting against Satan in heaven in Rev 12:7. He is shown fighting Satan on earth in Dan 12:1. The fighting on earth is the great tribulation. Although Michael will protect the 144,000 until the end of this time, Christians who hold to their faith will be slaughtered. This will be the time of great apostasy. When the beast is able to overcome God's witnesses, it will be because Michael has been removed from the fight. If Michael were not removed, the war between him and Satan would have brought about the extinction of mankind.

8   And their dead bodies shall lie in the street of the great city, which spiritually is called Sodom and Egypt, where also our Lord was crucified.

The great city where Jesus was crucified was Jerusalem. Later, Jerusalem will be referred to as "Babylon the Great."

> **9** **And they of the people and kindreds and tongues and nations shall see their dead bodies three days and an half, and shall not suffer their dead bodies to be put in graves.**

Although Jesus foretold that he would be resurrected from the grave, nobody understood or believed him. His dead body was put in a cave, hidden from view. In the same manner, these 144,000 witnesses of Jesus will prophesy that they will be raised back to life. Antichrist will kill them, but he will not allow them to be buried. He will keep them visible in order to disprove their resurrection prophecy.

> **10** **And they that dwell upon the earth shall rejoice over them, and make merry, and shall send gifts one to another; because these two prophets tormented them that dwelt on the earth.**

The people will rejoice because they survive. Matt. 24:22 says that if those days were not shortened (by the death of the 2 witnesses), no flesh would be saved (left alive). After this time, Christianity will be virtually non-existent.

This will be the time antichrist is revealed for who he is. This is when he will sit in the temple of God, declaring that he is God.

> **11** **And after three days and an half the Spirit of life from God entered into them, and they stood upon their feet; and great fear fell upon them which saw them.**
> **12** **And they heard a great voice from heaven saying unto them, Come up here. And they ascended up to heaven in a cloud; and their enemies beheld them.**

"Come up here" is the "trump of God," the third and final warning sound of 1 Thes 4:16. "For the Lord himself shall descend from heaven with a shout, with the voice of the archangel, and with the trump of God: and the dead in Christ shall rise first." The shout was likely Rev 9:14 "...Loose the four angels which are bound in the great river Euphrates." This will be followed by the voice of the archangel. Rev 10:3 "And cried with a loud voice, as when a lion roars: and when he had cried, seven thunders uttered their voices." "Come up here," will be the voice that causes the 2 witnesses to rise into heaven after the great tribulation. Only after these things have occurred will Jesus descend from heaven.

13 And the same hour was there a great earthquake, and the tenth part of the city fell, and in the earthquake were slain of men seven thousand: and the remnant were frightened, and gave glory to the God of heaven.

This is the same earthquake that began the 6th seal in Rev 6:12. A comparison between the 6th seal and Matt 24:29 confirms that this earthquake ends the great tribulation.

This is the end of the time when the great influx of martyrs will be found in heaven as told in Rev 7:9. "After this I beheld, and, lo, a great multitude, which no man could number, of all nations, and kindreds, and people, and tongues, stood before the throne, and before the Lamb, clothed with white robes, and palms in their hands;" and Rev 7:14 "...These are they which came out of the great tribulation..." It is these who spoke in the 5th seal. Rev 6:10-11.

> 10 And they cried with a loud voice, saying, How long, O Lord, holy and true, do you not judge and avenge our blood on them that dwell on the earth?
> 11 And white robes were given unto every one of them; and it was said unto them, that they should rest yet for a little season, until their fellow servants also and their brethren, that should be killed as they were, should be fulfilled.

Repentance, the call of John the Baptist, and the command of Jesus to the churches; will not be practiced in the Middle East after the invasion of the 200 million cavalry as found in Rev 9:20-21.

God does not want any to perish, but desires that all find eternal life. From verse 13 of this chapter, we find that the resurrection of the witnesses causes the unrepentant to give glory to God. The great falling away from the faith will end when the 2 witnesses are raised. Although Christianity will have been nearly wiped out, people will still receive salvation even at this short interval before Jesus returns! In order to combat this revival, this will likely be when the second beast of Chapter 13 will arise. He will be the false prophet that causes the mark of the beast.

It would not surprise me if the 7,000 who will die in the earthquake are the number of soldiers who will guard the 144,000 dead bodies.

14 The second woe is past; and, behold, the third woe comes quickly.

The 2nd woe began with 200 million cavalry gathering at the Euphrates River during the 6th trumpet. It will end under the reign of the antichrist. Antichrist will first gain power over Seleucia and then over 10 nations from the former Roman Empire. He and his empire will be more formally introduced in the 13th Chapter.

The end of the great tribulation will end the 1,260 days of verse 3. It will also be near the end of the 7 year period of time found in Dan 9:27. However, another 75 days are mentioned. Dan 12:11-12 "And from the time that the daily sacrifice shall be taken away, and the abomination that makes desolate set up, there shall be a thousand two hundred and ninety days. Blessed is he that waits, and comes to the thousand three hundred and five and thirty days." There will be 1,335 days from the beginning of the great tribulation until the final plague of hail has ended. (1,335 – 1,260 = 75)

It is Jesus who warns his church that he will "come quickly." In this context, Jesus will bring his wrath with him. The wrath of God will be found in Chapter 16.

15 And the seventh angel sounded; and there were great voices in heaven, saying, The kingdoms of this world are

become the kingdoms of our Lord, and of his Christ: and he shall reign for ever and ever.

God gave world leadership to Gentiles beginning with the Kingdom of Babylon under King Nebuchadnezzar. Gentile governance will continue through the time of the new Roman Empire. After that, the times of the Gentiles will be fulfilled and Jesus will reign forever.

16 **And the four and twenty elders, which sat before God on their seats, fell upon their faces, and worshipped God,**

17 **Saying, We give you thanks, O Lord God Almighty, which is, and was, and is to come; because you have taken your great power, and have begun to reign.**

18 **And the nations were angry, and your wrath is come, and the time of the dead, that they should be judged, and that you should give reward unto your servants the prophets, and to the saints, and them that fear your name, small and great; and should destroy they which destroy the earth.**

19 **And the temple of God was opened in heaven, and there was seen in his temple the ark of his testament: and there were lightnings, and voices, and thunderings, and an earthquake, and great hail.**

In the 6th seal, 5 events were shown:
A first great earthquake
The sun, moon, star event
Disappearance of the physical heaven
Appearance of the spiritual heaven
God's wrath which includes a second great earthquake

Verse 13 is the 1st great earthquake. The sun, moon, star event and the disappearance of the physical heaven is not mentioned here, but in verse 19, spiritual heaven is opened. Following this, God's wrath is revealed with the 2nd great earthquake and great hail. This unchanging sequence continues to provide understanding of the timing of events throughout the Revelation.

Chapter 12

There are 2 separate event sequences in this chapter. Verses 1-5 refer to the time of Jesus on earth. Verse 6 jumps to the future, the time of the abomination of desolation, the start of the great tribulation. As stated earlier, verses 7-17 refer to the times of the trumpets. Verse 14 is a repeat of verse 6. Both event sequences are in order, but there is a gap in time of almost 2,000 years between verses 5 and 6.

1 And there appeared a great wonder in heaven; a woman clothed with the sun, and the moon under her feet, and upon her head a crown of twelve stars:

When the wise men came from the east to see Jesus upon his birth, I believe they first saw this star configuration in the sky. The nation of Israel is represented, just as was revealed in Jacobs dream. Jacob was one of 12 brothers, the sons of Israel.

Gen. 37:9-10
9 ...the sun and the moon and the eleven stars made obeisance to me.
10 ...Shall I and your mother and your brothers indeed come to bow down ourselves to you to the earth?

2 And she being with child cried, travailing in birth, and pained to be delivered.

All of creation is in travail awaiting redemption of our physical bodies as revealed in the 1st seal. However, the pangs of this verse refer to the clash with Gentile leaders about the physical birth of Jesus, a new king in Israel according to prophecy.

3 And there appeared another wonder in heaven; and behold a great red dragon, having seven heads and ten horns, and seven crowns upon his heads.

Similar images will be seen in Chapters 13 and 17. The great red dragon is Satan. The 7 heads represent 7 kings or kingdoms that will or have ruled over Israel. The 10 horns are 10 kings who will be part of the leadership team in place when Jesus returns. The 10 kings don't have crowns in this vision because they are for a future time. The crowns are upon the heads because the 6th head or kingdom was ruling over Israel at the time of the vision. It was a vision for the time of Jesus' birth.

4 And his tail drew the third part of the stars of heaven, and did cast them to the earth: and the dragon stood before the woman which was ready to be delivered, for to devour her child as soon as it was born.

The stars once again represent angels. At the time Jesus was born, Satan and his angels influenced the government of Rome to try to kill Jesus. Herod killed all males under the age of 2 in the region Jesus was to be born. This account can be found in Matt. 2:13-16.

5 And she brought forth a man child, who was to rule all nations with a rod of iron: and her child was caught up unto God, and to his throne.

Jesus was born, died, and rose into heaven.

6 And the woman fled into the wilderness, where she has a place prepared of God, that they should feed her there a thousand two hundred and threescore days.

After the resurrection of Jesus, the nation of Israel was forced to flee from the Romans. However, Israel did not have a place prepared by God at that time. This part of the vision is separated from its beginning.

Verse 14 of this chapter says the woman was given the 2 wings of a great eagle to be nourished for the same 1,260 days. The 2 witnesses of Chapter 11, also known as the 144,000, will lead the people of Israel to the wilderness at the time of the abomination of desolation. There, they will be protected by the witnesses for 1,260 days during the great tribulation.

There was a previous time when the people of Israel fled into the wilderness following 2 witnesses named Moses and Aaron. It took them 40 years to make it to the Promised Land from Egypt.

As stated earlier, "Some of the events of Chapters 8 and 9 of the Revelation will also be seen in Chapter 12. The more physical aspects of the events were listed in the earlier chapters, while the more spiritual aspects will be listed now. There will be world war on earth; there will be heavenly war in 12:7. There will be no place for Satan and his angels in heaven in 12:8, and a great city will be destroyed on earth. The fall of the Wormwood star and the third part of the stars darkened is comparable to the fall of Satan with his angels in 12:9." Woe from Rev 8:13 compares with woe from Rev 12:12.

7　And there was war in heaven: Michael and his angels fought against the dragon; and the dragon fought and his angels,

8　And prevailed not; neither was their place found any more in heaven.

9　And the great dragon was cast out, that old serpent, called the Devil, and Satan, which deceives the whole world: he was cast out into the earth, and his angels were cast out with him.

10　And I heard a loud voice saying in heaven, Now is come salvation, and strength, and the kingdom of our God, and the power of his Christ: for the accuser of our brethren is cast down, which accused them before our God day and night.

11　And they overcame him by the blood of the Lamb, and by the word of their testimony; and they loved not their lives unto the death.

Apparently our salvation is not complete even when we have died and gone to heaven. It will become finalized when Satan is no longer in heaven to accuse us.

12 Therefore rejoice, you heavens, and you that dwell in them. Woe to the inhabiters of the earth and of the sea! For the devil is come down unto you, having great wrath, because he knows that he has but a short time.

13 And when the dragon saw that he was cast unto the earth, he persecuted the woman which brought forth the man child.

The 5th and 6th trumpets described the earthly forces Satan will use to persecute Israel; helicopters firing poison gas for 5 months, and then 200 million cavalry will damage Israel like a flood.

14 And to the woman were given two wings of a great eagle, that she might fly into the wilderness, into her place, where she is nourished for a time, and times, and half a time, from the face of the serpent.

15 And the serpent cast out of his mouth water as a flood after the woman, that he might cause her to be carried away of the flood.

16 And the earth helped the woman, and the earth opened her mouth, and swallowed up the flood which the dragon cast out of his mouth.

200 million against God's chosen people will not be enough. They will die trying to kill the people of Israel, just as Pharaoh's armies died chasing the Israelites when they left Egypt.

17 And the dragon was wroth with the woman, and went to make war with the remnant of her seed, which keep the commandments of God, and have the testimony of Jesus Christ.

Having failed to kill the Israelites, Satan will next try to kill Christians.

Chapter 13

1 And I stood upon the sand of the sea, and saw a beast rise up out of the sea, having seven heads and ten horns, and upon his horns ten crowns, and upon his heads the name of blasphemy.

In Chapter 7, the 4 winds were kept from stirring up the beast from the sea until the 144,000 people of Israel became Christians.

In contrast to the vision of the last chapter, the crowns are now upon the 10 horns. The 10 horns represent 10 kings that will form the new Roman Empire. This will be the kingdom which governs Israel at the time of Jesus' return as told in the 7th chapter of Daniel. The 7th head will be the first leader of the 10 nation union. This leader will make a holy 7 year covenant with Israel. We will be shown in Chapter 17 that antichrist will be an 8th head who will come to rule over the 10 nations.

2 And the beast which I saw was like unto a leopard, and his feet were as the feet of a bear, and his mouth as the mouth of a lion: and the dragon gave him his power, and his seat, and great authority.

These animal symbols show that this government is part of the 4 government structure pictured in chapters 2 and 7 of the book of Daniel. The 10 nation union of verse 1 represents the new version of the Roman Empire. It will be in power when Jesus returns. The leopard was Greece, the bear was Medo-Persia, and the lion was Babylon. Satan used these governments to persecute Israel.

3 And I saw one of his heads as it were wounded to death; and his deadly wound was healed: and all the world wondered after the beast.

The 5th trumpet revealed a leader that will arise from the area to the north of Israel representing part of the Greek Kingdom, namely

Seleucia. This same leader or government will again arise after the defeat of the 200 million cavalry. People will be amazed that another leader will come from this area after such a horrific defeat. This leader, the antichrist will not make, but he will confirm the 7 year holy covenant with the new 10 nation Roman government and the nation of Israel. The northern leader or antichrist will take over the new Roman government and rule the world for 42 months.

4   And they worshipped the dragon which gave power unto the beast: and they worshipped the beast, saying, Who is like unto the beast? Who is able to make war with him?

5   And there was given unto him a mouth speaking great things and blasphemies; and power was given unto him to continue forty and two months.

Just as the 2 witnesses will be given the spirit and power of Elijah, antichrist will first be given the spirit and power of Antiochus Epiphanes and then the spirit and power of a Roman Emperor. The northern leader or antichrist will eventually think of himself as a god. He will call himself God as he sits in the temple of God after he has defeated the 2 witnesses.

6   And he opened his mouth in blasphemy against God, to blaspheme his name, and his tabernacle, and them that dwell in heaven.

7   And it was given unto him to make war with the saints, and to overcome them: and power was given him over all kindreds, and tongues, and nations.

As stated in Chapter 11, this time of war between this antichrist and the 144,000, will be the time of the great tribulation. All nations will seek to kill Christians!

8   And all that dwell upon the earth shall worship him, whose names are not written in the book of life of the Lamb slain from the foundation of the world.

9   If any man have an ear, let him hear.

10 He that leads into captivity shall go into captivity: he that kills with the sword must be killed with the sword. Here is the patience and the faith of the saints.

This message is for every church. This saying was given to each church in Chapters 2 and 3. The Holy Spirit gives us ears to hear. Christians will be targeted for jail and/or death during this time. As a result of the persecution, many will fall away from the faith as stated in Chapter 11.

11 And I beheld another beast coming up out of the earth; and he had two horns like a lamb, and he spoke as a dragon.

At the end of "the great tribulation," when the 144,000 are raised from the dead, Christianity will be revived. Satan will counter this revival by releasing another angel from the place of the dead. This angel will influence a new beast or false prophet who will contradict the teachings of the 144,000.

Just as the 10 horns represent 10 kings or governments, these 2 horns represent 2 kings or governments. In the past, the 2 horns represented the combined government of Medo-Persia as found in the 8th chapter of Daniel. The modern form of this government is Iran. Coincidently, Iran is looking for a 12th Mahdi, the equivalent of an Islamic Messiah – possibly the false prophet.

12 And he exercises all the power of the first beast before him, and causes the earth and them which dwell therein to worship the first beast, whose deadly wound was healed.

Satan will give this false prophet, the same authority and miracle working abilities as antichrist. The false prophet will order people to worship antichrist, the leader who will miraculously be alive after defeat in the first woe.

13 And he does great wonders, so that he makes fire come down from heaven on the earth in the sight of men.

This is the same power that the 2 witnesses will have. This may refer to a modern air force.

14 **And deceives them that dwell on the earth by the means of those miracles which he had power to do in the sight of the beast; saying to them that dwell on the earth, that they should make an image to the beast, which had the wound by a sword, and did live.**

15 **And he had power to give life unto the image of the beast, that the image of the beast should both speak, and cause that as many as would not worship the image of the beast should be killed.**

16 **And he causes all, both small and great, rich and poor, free and bond, to receive a mark in their right hand, or in their foreheads:**

17 **And that no man might buy or sell, save he that had the mark, or the name of the beast, or the number of his name.**

18 **Here is wisdom. Let him that has understanding count the number of the beast: for it is the number of a man; and his number is Six hundred threescore and six.**

This second beast will persecute those who repent at the resurrection of the 144,000. Those who stay true to Jesus will not be able to participate in the economy from shortly after the time of the resurrection of the 144,000 until 1,335 days after the abomination of desolation. This will likely be 75 days at the most. Dan 12:10-12.

10 Many shall be purified, and made white, and tried; but the wicked shall do wickedly: and none of the wicked shall understand; but the wise shall understand.

11 And from the time that the daily sacrifice shall be taken away, and the abomination that makes desolate set up, there shall be a thousand two hundred and ninety days.

12 Blessed is he that waits, and comes to the thousand three hundred and five and thirty days.

People who will receive the 666 mark of the beast will be authorized by the government to eat, drink and be married. They will be surprised when God kills them in judgment. They are compared to the people of Noah's day in Matt. 24:38-39. "For as in the days that were before the flood they were eating and drinking, marrying and giving in marriage, until the day that Noah entered into the ark. And knew not until the flood came, and took them all away…"

Those who will refuse to take the mark of the beast will be taken during the judgment of the false prophet. His forces will go from business to business, killing those who will not accept the mark of the beast. These are pictured in Matt 24:40-43.

40 Then shall two be in the field; the one shall be taken, and the other left.
41 Two women shall be grinding at the mill; the one shall be taken, and the other left.
42 Watch therefore: for ye know not what hour your Lord will come.
43 But know this, that if the Goodman of the house had known in what watch the thief would come, he would have watched, and would not have suffered his house to be broken up.

If you have survived until the 144,000 are raised from the dead, it will be time for you and your family to quit your jobs or prepare for martyrdom. Satan will be coming to kill you.

This will be the last time of Christian martyrs. These receive special mention in Rev 20:4. "…and I saw the souls of them that were beheaded for the witness of Jesus, and for the word of God, and which had not worshipped the beast, neither his image, neither had received his mark upon their foreheads, or in their hands; and they lived and reigned with Christ a thousand years." These will be the people "taken" or killed by the false prophet. The one who is "left" will receive the mark.

Those who help others escape from the government of antichrist and his false prophet and survive throughout this period of time will obtain the kingdom of God.

Matt 25:31-40

31 When the Son of man shall come in his glory, and all the holy angels with him, then shall he sit upon the throne of his glory:

32 And before him shall be gathered all nations: and he shall separate them one from another, as a shepherd divides his sheep from the goats:

33 And he shall set the sheep on his right hand but the goats on the left.

34 Then shall the King say unto them on his right hand, Come, you blessed of my Father, inherit the kingdom prepared for you from the foundation of the world:

35 For I was hungry, and you gave me meat: I was thirsty, and you gave me drink: I was a stranger, and you took me in:

36 Naked, and you clothed me: I was sick, and you visited me: I was in prison, and you came unto me.

37 Then shall the righteous answer him, saying, Lord, when did we see you hungry, and fed you? Or thirsty, and gave you a drink?

38 When did we see you as a stranger, and took you in? or naked, and clothed you?

39 Or when did we see you sick, or in prison, and came to you?

40 And the King shall answer and say unto them, Verily I say unto you, Inasmuch as you have done it unto one of the least of these my brethren, you have done it unto me.

Chapter 14

1   And I looked, and, lo, a Lamb stood on the mount Zion, and with him an hundred forty and four thousand, having his Father's name written in their foreheads.

In this vision, the final act in the story of the 144,000 Messianic Jews will be played out. Act 1 from Chapter 7, introduced them as Israelites who will come to salvation in Jesus before the rise of the new Roman Empire. Act 2 was found in Chapter 11, where they were shown as 2 witnesses or 2 churches in the land of Israel. Here in Act 3, they become visible in heaven with Jesus.

Consistent with other passages, at the 1st great earthquake, the 144,000 will come back to life and their bodies will be lifted into the sky. Since a visible body raised from the dead and visibly lifted into the sky has only happened to Jesus, this will be "the sign of the Son of man" from Matt 24:30. Next, the physical heaven will depart and spiritual heaven will be revealed. When the 144,000 are visible in spiritual heaven, they will be "the sign of the Son of man in heaven."

2   And I heard a voice from heaven, as the voice of many waters, and of the voice of a great thunder: and I heard the voice of harpers harping with their harps:
3   And they sung as it were a new song before the throne, and before the four beasts, and the elders: and no man could learn that song but the hundred and forty and four thousand, which were redeemed from the earth.

In this picture, the Temple in heaven has opened, and the 144,000 have moved inside to a place before the throne. This will be the time of the 7th trumpet, the time that marks the beginning of Jesus' reign on earth. At this time antichrist will not have been destroyed. The Ark of the Covenant will be seen in the Temple as revealed in Rev 11:19.

There was a new song in Rev 5:9 when Jesus was raised into heaven and there will be a new song when the 144,000 are raised into heaven. It seems every time something new happens in heaven, there is new song that fits the occasion.

4   These are they which were not defiled with woman; for they are virgins. These are they which follow the Lamb wherever he goes. These were redeemed from among men, being the first fruits unto God and to the Lamb.

These will be men, probably young men since they will be virgins. They may form an army since they will protect the people of Israel in the wilderness and because the beast of the bottomless pit will make war against them.

This resurrection will be the first since Jesus' resurrection! These 2 witnesses will be called first fruits of the resurrection harvest as was Jesus. 1 Cor. 15:20 "But now is Christ risen from the dead, and become the firstfruits of them that slept." By naming them first fruits, the rest of the dead must come to life after this event. There can not be a resurrection in Chapter 4. Therefore, there can not be a rapture in Chapter 4!

There will be a resurrection of all who belong to Jesus in Chapter 20.

5   And in their mouth was found no guile: for they are without fault before the throne of God.

Satan, the accuser of the brethren has been cast out of heaven by this time, so they will be found not guilty in heaven.

6   And I saw another angel fly in the midst of heaven, having the everlasting gospel to preach unto them that dwell on the earth, and to every nation, and kindred, and tongue, and people.
7   Saying with a loud voice, Fear God, and give glory to him; for the hour of his judgment is come: and worship

him that made heaven, and earth, and the sea, and the fountains of waters.

Until this time, people will not only be unrepentant, but they will rejoice at the death of Christians, especially the 144,000. Rev 11:10 "And they that dwell upon the earth shall rejoice over them, and make merry, and shall send gifts one to another; because these two prophets tormented them that dwelt on the earth."

In keeping with the 5 events of the 6th seal, the 4th event was the visibility of spiritual heaven which has just been shown. The 5th event will be God's judgment or wrath which will be chronicled in Chapter 16. Those who accept Jesus and die before the death of the 2 witnesses will be kept out of the time of the wrath of God.

There will be those who accept Jesus as Lord and Savior after the 2 witnesses are raised from the dead. Rev 11:13 "…and in the earthquake were slain of men seven thousand: and the remnant were affrighted, and gave glory to the God of heaven." These people will face the "hour of judgment" or wrath of God because they will have forsaken the word of God prior to the resurrection of the 144,000. This time was foreshadowed in the message to Philadelphia, Rev 3:7-10. Although the temple in heaven will be closed during the period of God's wrath, the spirits of God's people killed during this time will not be lost. Matt 24:31 "…they shall gather together his elect from the four winds, from one end of heaven to the other."

After the great martyrdom and great apostasy, an angel will perform the great commission. This angel may represent a star or satellite. Either by angel or by satellite, the salvation message will once again go out into all the earth. Matt 24:14 "And this gospel of the kingdom shall be preached in all the world for a witness unto all nations; and then shall the end come."

8 And there followed another angel, saying, Babylon is fallen, is fallen, that great city, because she made all nations drink of the wine of the wrath of her fornication.

Babylon, the great city, in this context will be earthly Jerusalem. It will be there that Antichrist will have an image of himself to be worshipped. From Jerusalem, Satan will cause all governments to kill Christians. Rev 17:6 "And I saw the woman drunken with the blood of the saints, and with the blood of the martyrs of Jesus…"

9   **And the third angel followed them, saying with a loud voice, If any man worship the beast and his image, and receive his mark in his forehead, or in his hand,**

10 **The same shall drink of the wine of the wrath of God, which is poured out with mixture into the cup of his indignation; he shall be tormented with fire and brimstone in the presence of the holy angels, and in the presence of the Lamb:**

11 **And the smoke of their torment ascends up for ever and ever: and they have no rest day nor night, who worship the beast and his image, and who ever receives the mark of his name.**

The wrath of Satan can kill the body, but the wrath of God can kill the body and the soul. Those who follow Satan and the beast will not only die on earth, but they will be tormented forever. Once the mark of the beast is taken in the forehead or right hand, only one teaching provides hope. Matt 5:29-30 "And if your right eye offends you, pluck it out, and cast it from you: for it is profitable for you that one of your members should perish, and not that your whole body should be cast into hell. And if your right hand offends you, cut it off, and cast it from you: for it is profitable for you that one of your members should perish, and not that your whole body should be cast into hell." There is no way of knowing if cutting off your hand or plucking out your eye (ridding yourself of the mark of the beast) will accomplish bringing you back into God's grace. The safest way to ensure this is to never take the mark of the beast.

12 **Here is the patience of the saints: here are they that keep the commandments of God, and the faith of Jesus.**

13 **And I heard a voice from heaven saying unto me, Write, Blessed are the dead which die in the Lord from**

henceforth: Yea, says the Spirit, that they may rest from the labors; and their works do follow them.

As was pointed out in the last chapter, those who keep faith in Jesus until death during this period of time will receive special recognition in the resurrection in Rev 20:4.

14 And I looked, and behold a white cloud, and upon the cloud one sat like unto the Son of man, having on his head a golden crown, and in his hand a sharp sickle.

There will not be any more signs of Jesus' return because this will be his return. He will come as he left; on a cloud. In Chapter 19, this cloud will be called a white horse.

In this vision, Jesus will be riding on the smoke filled Temple of God in heaven and will be on his way to earth. The dead in Christ will not be able to come into the temple at this time.

15 And another angel came out of the temple, crying with a loud voice to him that sat on the cloud, Thrust in your sickle, and reap: for the time is come for you to reap; for the harvest of the earth is ripe.

1 Thes 4:16 "For the Lord himself shall descend from heaven with a shout, with the voice of the archangel, and with the trump of God: and the dead in Christ shall rise first." We have seen the shout, the voice, and the trump. Now we learn that the dead in Christ will not be raised until God's wrath has been poured out.

This sickle of God is the same sickle that will be in the hands of the false prophet, beheading Christians. Those killed are pictured in Rev 15:2. "And I saw as it were a sea of glass mingled with fire: and them that had gotten the victory over the beast, and over his image, and over his mark, and over the number of his name, stand on the sea of glass, having the harps of God." Having a harp of God is redemption from the earth, but not bodily resurrection. Again, all of these people will come to faith in Jesus after the 2 witnesses have been raised; in spite of the efforts of the false prophet.

16 And he that sat on the cloud thrust in his sickle on the earth; and the earth was reaped.

This is comparable to the early or spring harvest and was foreshadowed in the 3rd seal. Christians will be harvested first and will have to work all day to eat, while non-Christians will be harvested later and will have plenty.

17 And another angel came out of the temple which is in heaven, he also having a sharp sickle.
18 And another angel came out from the altar, which had power over fire; and cried with a loud cry to him that had the sharp sickle, saying, Thrust in your sharp sickle, and gather the clusters of the vine of the earth; for her grapes are fully ripe.
19 And the angel thrust in his sickle into the earth, and gathered the vine of the earth, and cast it into the great winepress of the wrath of God.
20 And the winepress was trodden without the city, and blood came out of the winepress, even unto the horse bridles, by the space of a thousand and six hundred furlongs.

The late or fall harvest of unbelievers is pictured here and in Rev 16:19. "…And great Babylon came in remembrance before God, to give unto her the cup of the wine of the fierceness of his wrath." It is also pictured in Rev 19:21. "And the remnant were slain with the sword of him that sat upon the horse, which sword proceeded out of his mouth: and all the fowls were filled with their flesh."

God's people will be killed because of orders given from Jerusalem. As a result, God will avenge their deaths by killing the armies of the whole world just outside of that same city.

Chapter 15

1   And I saw another sign in heaven, great and marvelous, seven angels having the seven last plagues; for in them is filled up the wrath of God.

In the 6th seal and in the 24th chapter of Matthew, stars fall after the sun and moon are darkened. The first chapter revealed that stars are symbols of angels. This portent will likely be 7 falling or shooting stars. In sequence, the 2 witnesses will be raised from the dead, there will be a great earthquake, the sun and moon will be darkened, and then this sign in the stars will appear. The sky will then disappear and spiritual heaven will become visible.

Rev 6:13 "And the stars of heaven fell unto the earth…" Rev 6:14 "And the heaven departed as a scroll…"

2   And I saw as it were a sea of glass mingled with fire: and them that had gotten the victory over the beast, and over his image, and over his mark, and over the number of his name, stand on the sea of glass, having the harps of God.

As part of God's wrath, Jesus will reap the earth as told in verses 14-16 of Chapter 14. Victorious Christians, those killed during the time of the false prophet; will be gathered by angels and taken before the throne of God. Unlike the 144,000, their bodies will still be waiting for the resurrection. We know they will be in spiritual heaven because the sea of glass was mentioned in Rev 4:6. "And before the throne there was a sea of glass like unto crystal…"

3   And they sing the song of Moses the servant of God, and the song of the Lamb, saying, Great and marvelous are your works, Lord God Almighty; just and true are your ways, you King of saints.

4   Who shall not fear you, O Lord, and glorify your name: for you only are holy: for your judgments are made manifest.

People of Israel and people of Gentile nations who will be killed by the beast will find their place in heaven.

God's judgments made manifest are not signs. They will have happened at this point. As has often been the case, a new sequence of events will be shown that will fill in more details about this end time sequence.

5   And after that I looked, and, behold, the temple of the tabernacle of the testimony in heaven was opened:

This is part of a new vision that will occur before the 7 last plagues of God's judgment are made manifest.

After the stars fall, heaven will be shaken and the sky will vanish. This will enable the people on earth to view not only Jesus with the 144,000; but also the Holy of Holies, the Most Holy Place in heaven. The tabernacle of testimony is the tent where the 10 Commandments are kept, the Most Holy Place. Jesus will be anointed as King at this time, fulfilling the 7th trumpet in Rev 11:15. "The kingdoms of this world are become the kingdoms of our Lord, and of his Christ; and he shall reign for ever and ever. This anointing will be the final segment of the seventy weeks mentioned in Dan 9:24. "Seventy weeks are determined upon thy people and upon thy holy city, to finish the transgression, and to make an end of sins, and to make reconciliation for iniquity, and to bring in everlasting righteousness, and to seal up the vision and prophecy, and to anoint the most Holy."

6   And the seven angels came out of the temple, having the seven plagues, clothed in pure and white linen, and having their breasts girded with golden girdles.
7   And one of the four beasts gave unto the seven angels seven golden vials full of the wrath of God, who lives for ever and ever.

8 And temple was filled with smoke from the glory of God, and from his power; and no man was able to enter into the temple, till the seven plagues of the seven angels were fulfilled.

After the 144,000 have entered the temple in heaven, no one else will be able to enter. This is what is pictured in the parable of the 10 virgins in Matt 25.

1 Then shall the kingdom of heaven be likened unto ten virgins, which took their lamps, and went forth to meet the bridegroom.
2 And five of them were wise, and five were foolish.
3 They that were foolish took their lamps, and took no oil with them:
4 But the wise took oil in their vessels with their lamps.
5 While the bridegroom tarried, they all slumbered and slept.
6 And at midnight there was a cry made, Behold, the bridegroom comes; go you out to meet him.
7 Then all those virgins arose, and trimmed their lamps.
8 And the foolish said unto the wise, Give us of your oil; for our lamps are gone out.
9 But the wise answered, saying, Not so; lest there be not enough for us and you: but go rather to them that sell, and buy for yourselves.
10 And while they went to buy, the bridegroom came; and they that were ready went in with him to the marriage: and the door was shut.

This is a preview of the marriage supper of the Lamb which is coming in Rev 19:6-9. Everyone who belongs to Jesus will forever be joined with him at this time. The foolish virgins, those who will fall away from the faith during the time of the false prophet, may still become part of the first resurrection if they are killed for their faith. Those who do not know Jesus at his coming may still obtain the kingdom because they will be doing God's will unaware as pictured in the sheep and goat parable of Matt 25:31-46.

Chapter 16

1 And I heard a great voice out of the temple saying to the seven angels, Go your ways, and pour out the vials of the wrath of God upon the earth.

The vials of God's wrath that were "made manifest" in the last chapter will now be identified.

2 And the first went, and poured out his vial upon the earth; and there fell a noisome and grievous sore upon the men which had the mark of the beast, and upon them which worshipped his image.

Before receiving the mark of the beast, people will have to honor the beast as God. Everyone who participates in the economy after the false prophet appears on the scene will have accepted the 666 mark. At this time, the mark on the hand or on the forehead will become infected.

3 And the second angel poured out his vial upon the sea; and it became as the blood of a dead man: and every living soul died in the sea.

The sea will become poisonous. In the seals, death from war, famine, pestilence, and the nations will be limited to 25% of the population. The death limit was raised to 33% at the time of the 6th trumpet. During the vial judgments, the time of God's wrath, all limits are off. The sea will not be a good place to hide from the wrath of God.

4 And the third angel poured out his vial upon the rivers and fountains of waters; and they became blood.
5 And I heard the angel of the waters say, You are righteous, O Lord, who is, and was, and will be, because you have judged thus.

6 For they have shed the blood of saints and prophets, and you have given them blood to drink; for they are worthy.

7 And I heard another out of the altar say, Even so, Lord God Almighty, true and righteous are your judgments.

The drinking water will become poisonous, although it may not become actual blood. During the 6th seal, when the moon became as blood, it was just red.

Retribution of this kind is not unprecedented. At the time of Moses, Egyptians killed the infants of Israel by drowning them in the Nile River. As a result, God turned the Nile River into blood. In verse 6 above, all nations will be guilty of killing God's people. As a result, God will make all rivers like the Nile during the Exodus.

8 And fourth angel poured out his vial upon the sun; and power was given unto him to scorch men with fire.

9 And men were scorched with great heat, and blasphemed the name of God, which has power over these plagues: and they repented not to give him glory.

Although this falling star will not hit the earth, its effects will be felt upon earth. Severe sunburn will come at this time. All of these plagues will come after spiritual heaven has become visible; therefore, all people will know the true God, and they will curse him.

10 And the fifth angel poured out his vial upon the seat of the beast; and his kingdom was full of darkness; and they gnawed their tongues for pain.

11 And blasphemed the God of heaven because of their pains and their sores, and repented not of their deeds.

It appears the sores and/or great sunshine will cause temporary blindness. Zeph 1:17 "And I will bring distress upon men, that they shall walk like blind men, because they have sinned against the Lord: and their blood shall be poured out as dust, and their flesh as the dung." The blindness will only be for a while because in the next vile, people will be on the move.

> **12 And the sixth angel poured out his vial upon the great river Euphrates; and the water thereof was dried up, that the way of the kings of the east might be prepared.**
> **13 And I saw three unclean spirits like frogs come out of the mouth of the dragon, and out of the mouth of the beast, and out of the mouth of the false prophet.**
> **14 For they are the spirits of devils, working miracles, which go forth unto the kings of the earth and of the whole world, to gather them to the battle of that great day of God Almighty.**

During the 6th trumpet, 4 angels were released at the Euphrates River to influence 200 million cavalry. At this time, 3 evil spirits will be able to influence the whole world to go to war. Satan, the spirit controlling antichrist, and the spirit controlling the false prophet; will be able convince people worldwide that their only hope is to defeat God when he comes to earth. There will not be any warships in the battle because the 2nd vial already killed everyone at sea.

> **15 Behold, I come as a thief. Blessed is he that watches, and keeps his garments, lest he walk naked, and they see his shame.**

Since the armies of the whole world will be gathering to fight against God, coming like a thief in this context does not mean that his coming will be a surprise. John 10:10 "The thief comes not, but for to steal, and to kill, and to destroy…" God will come as a thief against his enemies.

God is coming. Put on the righteousness of Christ and keep it. Your own righteousness will be put to shame in the presence of a Holy God.

> **16 And he gathered them together into a place called in the Hebrew tongue Armageddon.**

This is a place in Israel to the north of Jerusalem capable of being filled with vast armies.

> **17** **And the seventh angel poured out his vial into the air; and there came a great voice out of the temple of heaven, from the throne, saying, It is done.**
> **18** **And there were voices, and thunders, and lightnings; and there was a great earthquake, such as was not since men were upon the earth, so mighty an earthquake, and so great.**

The voices, thunders, and lightnings; are always shown to come from the throne of God in the Revelation. This will be the 2nd great earthquake of the end time sequence.

> **19** **And the great city was divided into three parts, and the cities of the nations fell: and great Babylon came in remembrance before God, to give unto her the cup of the wine of the fierceness of his wrath.**
> **20** **And every island fled away, and the mountains were not found.**

This earthquake will devastate and level the whole earth. This great earthquake was also revealed as part of the 6th seal.

> **21** **And there fell upon men a great hail out of heaven, every stone about the weight of a talent: and men blasphemed God because of the plague of the hail; for the plague thereof was exceeding great.**

Hail smashing the blood out of men is the great winepress or fall harvest of God pictured in Rev 14:19-20. This will be the great day of God's wrath from Rev 6:17. The noises in heaven followed by the earthquake and hail were also pictured after the trumpet sequence in Rev 11:19.

Chapter 17

1 And there came one of the seven angels which had the seven vials, and talked with me, saying unto me, Come here; I will show unto you the judgment of the great whore that sits upon many waters.

Although many symbols are defined, this chapter is still difficult to understand because the era of the symbol determines its definition. For instance, the Babylonian Empire was represented by a beast, but it was only 1 of 4 kingdoms represented as a beast. Additionally, the kingdom and the great city which governed the kingdom can share the same name. For example, Babylon the kingdom and Babylon the city are not distinguishable by name.

The great whore is defined in the 18th verse of this chapter. "And the woman which you saw is that great city, which reigns over the kings of the earth:" The woman, the whore, the harlot, Babylon the Great; whatever you want to call the woman, she is a city. For whatever reason, God's definition is seldom used. Three more times in Chapter 18, the whore will be called the great city because that is what it is! Rev 14:8 defined Babylon the same way. "…Babylon is fallen, is fallen, that great city…" The great cities of the world empires are contrasted with the new Jerusalem, the great city that will come down from heaven in Rev 21:2. "And I John saw the holy city, new Jerusalem, coming down from God out of heaven…"

There have been 4 world empires and the 4th one will return. Each of the world empires contains a great city which governs the empire. Therefore, the great whore can be a reference to the capital city of any of the 4 empires. The city of Rome was the great whore of the Roman Empire, the city that ruled during John's lifetime.

The waters are defined in verse 15. "…The waters which you saw, where the whore sits, are peoples, and multitudes, and nations, and tongues." The people governed by any of the 4 empires are the "waters."

The judgment of the great whore is delivered by ten horns as shown in verse 16. "And the ten horns which you saw upon the beast, these shall hate the whore, and shall make her desolate and naked, and shall eat her flesh, and burn her with fire." Since the 10 horns are 10 kings that will only be relevant in the new Roman Empire, the judgment shown will be upon the city of Rome, the future capital of the coming world empire. When Rome is destroyed, power will transfer from the city of Rome to the city of Jerusalem. This power transfer from the Roman leader to the antichrist was revealed in Rev 13:5. "And there was given unto him a mouth speaking great things and blasphemies; and power was given unto him to continue forty and two months."

As the final great whore, Jerusalem will also face judgment. That judgment will be shown in Chapters 18 and 19.

2   With whom the kings of the earth have committed fornication, and the inhabitants of the earth have been made drunk with the wine of her fornication.

Verse 6 defines the wine of the great whore that made the nations drunk. "And I saw the woman drunken with the blood of the saints, and with the blood of the martyrs of Jesus...." Wine is the blood of God's people, shed to please the great city.

The kings of the earth with their peoples, and multitudes, and nations, and tongues; will follow the lead of the great city and kill God's people. This was referred to in Rev 14:8-13, where Babylon is symbolic of end time Jerusalem.

3   So he carried me away in the spirit into the wilderness: and I saw a woman sit upon a scarlet colored beast, full of names of blasphemy, having seven heads and ten horns.

The spirit carried John to places from which he could see, hear, and write. Other places where this is found are Rev 1:10, 4:2, and 21:10.

The beast is defined in verses 8-14. It has names of blasphemy, that is, names that either deny God or claim to be God. Dan 7:17 and 23 define the beast as a king or a kingdom. Similar visions in Chapters 12 and 13 show crowns upon the heads or the horns. Seven heads or kings will rule over Israel. Four of those 7 kings ruled the 4 world empires. Two of the 7 were split off from the kingdom of Greece. The last of the 7 will rule the new Roman Empire. When the 10 king confederacy rules at the time of Jesus return, they will give their power and authority to an eighth king who will be the antichrist.

Since this vision is without crowns, it is a generic form of the kingdoms and great cities governing Israel over time.

4 And the woman was arrayed in purple and scarlet color, and decked with gold and precious stones and pearls, having a golden cup in her hand full of abominations and filthiness of her fornication:

The great city has the colors and treasures of a king. Jer 51:7 "Babylon has been a golden cup in the Lord's hand that made all the earth drunken: the nations have drunken of her wine; therefore the nations are mad." Once again, this is imagery of the nations killing the people of God under the direction of a great city.

5 And upon her forehead was a name written, MYSTERY, BABYLON THE GREAT, THE MOTHER OF HARLOTS AND ABOMINATIONS OF THE EARTH.

The actual city of Babylon was the first great city of the first great empire. Although God used the people of this city to punish Israel for its sin, Babylon was not without sin. For example, the city of Babylon caused the people of all cities in the kingdom to worship an image in the 3rd chapter of Daniel. Everyone in the Medo-

Persian kingdom was ordered to worship Darius the king for 30 days in the 6th chapter of Daniel.

The great city (Mother) causes people in all cities (Harlots) to sin. The sin that will bring ultimate judgment will be the order from the great city to kill God's people.

> **6 And I saw the woman drunken with the blood of the saints, and with the blood of the martyrs of Jesus: and when I saw her, I wondered with great admiration.**

The only city that fits this description to date is Rome. Jesus was born during the era of the Roman Empire. Rome had many Christians killed.

When John wonders about the woman, it is because she will be reborn as from the dead. In verse 8, the same wonder occurs for the same reason in regard to the beast.

Rome will once again be the great city that will rule the world in the new Roman Empire, but in the future she will not be the city responsible for killing God's people. That will occur when the future capital is moved to Jerusalem.

> **7 And the angel said unto me, Why did you marvel? I will tell you the mystery of the woman, and of the beast that carries her, which has the seven heads and ten horns.**
>
> **8 The beast that you saw was, and is not; and shall ascend out of the bottomless pit, and go into perdition: and they that dwell on the earth shall wonder, whose names were not written in the book of life from the foundation of the world, when they behold the beast that was, and is not, and yet is.**

This beast can not be symbolic of the Roman Empire because it was in power when John wrote the Revelation. Therefore, "Is not" of verse 8 was not applicable. This beast had to have authority previous to the Roman Empire.

The beast that will ascend from the bottomless pit was revealed in Chapter 9 as the Seleucid Kingdom. The first 2 forms of this kingdom will not become world empires, but the 3rd will eventually gain authority over the new Roman Empire.

9   And here is the mind which has wisdom. The seven heads are seven mountains, on which the woman sits.

Rome is the city of 7 mountains or 7 hills, and Rome was the great city of John's time.

10 And there are seven kings: five are fallen, and one is, and the other is not yet come; and when he comes, he must continue a short space.

The 7 kings or kingdoms come from the 4 world empires found in Daniel; from Babylon, Medo-Persia, Greece, and Rome.

In the 8th chapter of Daniel, 4 small kingdoms came from the kingdom of Greece. Two of them never ruled over Israel, but two did. The 2 that did were the kingdoms of Ptolemy and Seleucia. The 6 heads of history to the time of John were Babylon, Medo-Persia, Greece, Ptolemy, Seleucia, and Rome. The 7th head which will rule in Rome will recognize God's Holy Covenant with Israel and allow animal sacrifice to resume. He will only be in power for a short space. The nation of the 8th head (see verse 11 below), along with many others will confirm this covenant, as stated in Dan 9:27.

A continuous succession of kings from the same empire is only considered to be one head.

11 And the beast that was, and is not, even he is the eighth, and is of the seven, and goes into perdition.

John has the same wonder for the 8th head as he does for the whore. That wonder resulted from a governing power recovering authority after it has long been dead. Seleucia, the king to the north of Israel in the 11th chapter of Daniel, will be the 8th head. This head will also be known as antichrist.

12 And the ten horns which you saw are ten kings, which have received no kingdom as yet; but receive power as kings one hour with the beast.

The 10 kings or governments that will be in power when Jesus returns were not in power when John wrote the Revelation. They will be given authority after the 144,000 Israelites become Christians.

13 These have one mind, and shall give their power and strength unto the beast.

When the 10 receive their authority, they will soon give it to Seleucia. Just as the first leader of the new Roman Empire received authority for just a short space, the second leader will only reign for 42 months.

14 These shall make war with the Lamb, and the Lamb shall overcome them: for he is Lord of lords, and King of kings: and they that are with him are called, and chosen, and faithful.

All of the nations of the world will gather at Armageddon to battle against Jesus. Jesus will win! This will take place after the great tribulation, during the period of God's wrath.

15 And he said unto me, The waters which you saw, where the whore sits, are peoples, and multitudes, and nations, and tongues.

16 And the ten horns which you saw upon the beast, these shall hate the whore, and shall make her desolate and naked, and shall eat her flesh, and burn her with fire.

17 For God has put in their hearts to fulfill his will, and to agree, and give their kingdom unto the beast, until the words of God shall be fulfilled.

18 And the woman which you saw is that great city, which reigns over the kings of the earth.

The 10 kings of the new Roman Empire will destroy the city of Rome when they give their power to Seleucia. The capital of the new Roman Empire will then be transferred to the city of Jerusalem.

Chapter 18

1   **And after these things I saw another angel come down from heaven, having great power; and the earth was lightened with his glory.**

2   **And he cried mightily with a strong voice, saying, Babylon the great is fallen, is fallen, and is become the habitation of devils, and the hold of every foul spirit, and a cage of every unclean and hateful bird.**

3   **For all nations have drunk of the wine of the wrath of her fornication, and the kings of the earth have committed fornication with her, and the merchants of the earth are waxed rich through the abundance of her delicacies.**

This is repeated from Rev 14:8. Jerusalem is the great city that will cause all nations to kill Christians.

In review; when Satan is cast from heaven, he will try to wipe out the nation of Israel. God will protect some of Israel, so Satan will next attack Christians worldwide with the full power of the new Roman Empire. This will be the time of the great tribulation.

4   **And I heard another voice from heaven, saying, Come out of her, my people, that you be not partakers of her sins, and that you receive not of her plagues.**

5   **For her sins have reached unto heaven, and God has remembered her iniquities.**

"Coming out of her" will be to come out from under her authority. To be under her authority will be to kill Christians, to eventually take the mark of the beast, and to ultimately end up in the lake of fire.

Many Christians will be killed and many others will fall away from the faith during this time.

6   Reward her even as she rewarded you, and double unto her double according to her works: in the cup which she has filled fill to her double.

7   How much she has glorified herself, and lived deliciously, so much torment and sorrow give her: for she says in her heart, I sit a queen, and am no widow, and shall see no sorrow.

These will be the prayers of all saints which went up to God, pictured in the 7th seal, Rev 8:3-4.

This time the great city is compared to a queen instead of a harlot. The people of Jerusalem will believe in their husband, the king of the north or antichrist. They will not believe they will be judged until judgment comes. This is reminiscent of Noah's time. The people refused to believe the flood was coming until there was no escape.

8   Therefore shall her plagues come in one day, death, and mourning, and famine; and she shall be utterly burned with fire: for strong is the Lord God who judges her.

Being utterly burned with fire is a plague that is revealed in Zech 14:12. "And this shall be the plague wherewith the Lord will smite all the people that have fought against Jerusalem; Their flesh shall consume away while they stand upon their feet, and their eyes shall consume away in their holes, and their tongue shall consume away in their mouth."

9   And the kings of the earth, who have committed fornication and lived deliciously with her, shall bewail her, and lament for her, when they shall see the smoke of her burning.

10 Standing afar off for the fear of her torment, saying, Alas, alas that great city Babylon, that mighty city! For in one hour is your judgment come.

11 And the merchants of the earth shall weep and mourn over her; for no man buys their merchandise any more:

12 The merchandise of gold, and silver, and precious stone, and of pearls, and fine linen, and purple, and silk, and scarlet, and all thyine wood, and all manner vessels of ivory, and all manner vessels of most precious wood, and of brass, and iron, and marble,

13 And cinnamon, and odors, and ointments, and frankincense, and wine, and oil, and fine flour, and wheat, and beasts, and sheep, and horses, and chariots, and slaves, and souls of men.

14 And the fruits that your soul lusted after are departed from you, and all things which were dainty and goodly are departed from you, and you will find them no more at all.

15 The merchants of these things, which were made rich by her, shall stand afar off for the fear of her torment, weeping and wailing,

16 And saying, Alas, alas that great city, that was clothed in fine linen, and purple, and scarlet, and decked with gold, and precious stones, and pearls!

17 For in one hour so great riches is come to naught. And every shipmaster, and all the company in ships, and sailors, and as many as trade by sea, stood afar off,

18 And cried when they saw the smoke of her burning, saying, What city is like unto this great city!

19 And they cast dust on their heads, and cried, weeping and wailing, saying, Alas, alas that great city, wherein were made rich all that had ships in the sea by reason of her costliness! For in one hour is she made desolate.

These merchants will lose all of their wealth. Zech 14:14 "...and the wealth of all the heathen round about shall be gathered together, gold, and silver, and apparel, in great abundance."

20 Rejoice over her, you heaven, and you holy apostles and prophets; for God has avenged you on her.

Matt 23:37 "O Jerusalem, Jerusalem, you kill the prophets, and stone them which are sent unto you..."

In Rev 6:10, the martyrs asked, "How long, O Lord, holy and true, will you not judge and avenge our blood on them that dwell on the earth?" The 5th seal which began with the death of Stephen, the first martyr will be nearing its end when God's judgment and vengeance is brought upon Jerusalem. The first great earthquake that ends the period of great tribulation will be the beginning of God's judgment.

> 21 **And a mighty angel took up a stone like a great millstone, and cast it into the sea, saying, Thus with violence shall that great city Babylon be thrown down, and shall be found no more at all.**
>
> 22 **And the voice of harpers, and musicians, and of pipers, and trumpeters, shall be heard no more at all in you; and no craftsman, of whatsoever craft he be, shall be found any more in you; and the sound of a millstone shall be heard no more at all in you;**
>
> 23 **And the light of a candle shall shine no more at all in you; and the voice of the bridegroom and of the bride shall be heard no more at all in you: for your merchants were the great men of the earth; for by your sorceries were all nations deceived.**

When the people of Jerusalem are destroyed, God will begin his reign. This will be the day of the 7th trumpet from Rev 11:15. "…The kingdoms of this world are become the kingdoms of our Lord, and of his Christ; and he shall reign for ever and ever."

> 24 **And in her was found the blood of prophets, and of saints, and of all that were slain upon the earth.**

The people of Jerusalem that will be responsible for the killing of Christians will be utterly destroyed; however Jerusalem, the place and people of the living God will still exist. Zech 14:11 "And men shall dwell in it, and there shall be no more utter destruction; but Jerusalem shall be safely inhabited."

Chapter 19

1 And after these things I heard a great voice of much people in heaven, saying, Alleluia; Salvation, and glory, and honor, and power, unto the Lord our God:

This is the same picture of the great multitude that died during the great tribulation as found in Rev 7:9-15.

2 For true and righteous are his judgments: for he has judged the great whore, which did corrupt the earth with her fornication, and has avenged the blood of his servants at her hand.

God's judgment will include Jerusalem.

3 And again they said, Alleluia. And her smoke rose up for ever and ever.

All who receive the mark will be tormented forever. This was previously announced in Rev 14:9-11.

4 And the four and twenty elders and the four beasts fell down and worshipped God that sat on the throne, saying, Amen; Alleluia.

5 And a voice came out of the throne, saying, Praise our God, all you his servants, and you that fear him, both small and great.

6 And I heard as it were the voice of a great multitude, and as the voice of many waters, and as the voice of mighty thunderings, saying, Alleluia: for the Lord God omnipotent reigns.

7 Let us be glad and rejoice, and give honor to him: for the marriage of the Lamb is come, and his wife has made herself ready.

Even after God's judgment upon Jerusalem, only God's first fruits will have been physically raised from the dead. The rest of the dead who belong to Jesus will be spirits only. Both groups will be joined with Jesus forever.

Again we find the voices and thunderings which occur just before the 2nd great earthquake.

> **8 And to her was granted that she should be arrayed in fine linen, clean and white: for the fine linen is the righteousness of saints.**

The righteousness of saints is the blood of the Lamb as explained in Rev 7:14.

> **9 And he said unto me, Write, Blessed are they which are called unto the marriage supper of the Lamb. And he said unto me, These are the true sayings of God.**

Matt 22:2-10 pictures this time.

> 2 The kingdom of heaven is like unto a certain king, which made a marriage for his son,
>
> 3 And sent forth his servants to call them that were bidden to the wedding: and they would not come.
>
> 4 Again, he sent forth other servants, saying, Tell them which are bidden, Behold, I have prepared my dinner: my oxen and my fatlings are killed, and all things are ready: come unto the marriage.
>
> 5 But they made light of it, and went their ways, one to his farm, another to his merchandise:
>
> 6 And the remnant took his servants, and treated them spitefully, and slew them.
>
> 7 But when the king heard thereof, he was wroth: and he sent forth his armies, and destroyed those murderers, and burned up their city.
>
> 8 Then said he to his servants, The wedding is ready, but they which were bidden were not worthy.

9 Go therefore into the highways, and as many as you shall find, bid to the marriage.

10 So those servants went out into the highways, and gathered together all as many as they found, both bad and good: and the wedding was furnished with guests.

Just before the wedding comes, many Christians will fall away from the faith. Some of them will take the mark of the beast to participate in the economy, while others will kill those who remain true to Jesus. All of the faithless will be killed by God, and Jerusalem will be burned up. God will send his angels to gather to heaven the spirits of all who will die at this time. Those who have the righteousness of Jesus will stay. Those who don't belong in heaven will be cast out.

10 And I fell at his feet to worship him. And he said unto me, See you do it not: I am your fellow servant, and of your brethren that have the testimony of Jesus: worship God: for the testimony of Jesus is the spirit of prophecy.

11 And I saw heaven opened, and behold a white horse; and he that sat upon him was called Faithful and True, and in righteousness he does judge and make war.

Instead of moving forward from the voices and thunders to the 2nd great earthquake of the sequence, we move back in time to the point when the physical sky will be torn open to reveal the spiritual heaven. The details of Rev 14:1-13 are skipped, but Jesus will ride on a white cloud (white horse), just as he did in Rev 14:14. The wife of the lamb has been completed, but those who will die as Jesus harvests the earth will become wedding guests.

12 His eyes were as a flame of fire, and on his head were many crowns; and he had a name written, that no man knew, but he himself.

Jesus was first pictured upon a white horse in Rev 6:2 at the time he conquered sin and death. The many crowns are from all who humble themselves in surrender to Jesus.

In Rev 2:17, Christians are promised a stone with a new name. Here, Jesus likely has a similar stone.

13 And he was clothed with a vesture dipped in blood: and his name is called The Word of God.

14 And the armies which were in heaven followed him upon white horses, clothed in fine linen, white and clean.

The armies include the angels, the spirits of the dead in Christ, and the 144,000 who will have been resurrected.

15 And out of his mouth goes a sharp sword, that with it he should smite the nations: and he shall rule them with a rod of iron: and he treads the winepress of the fierceness and wrath of Almighty God.

The sword is the word of God. Just as has been written, Jesus will cause great hail to squash the blood out of men from all nations as with a winepress. This was also seen in Rev 16:21, after the 7th vial had been poured out.

16 And he has on his vesture and on his thigh a name written, KING OF KINGS, AND LORD OF LORDS.

Jesus will reign on earth. There will still be kings on earth, but none like Jesus.

17 And I saw an angel standing in the sun; and he cried with a loud voice, saying to all the fowls that fly in the midst of heaven, Come and gather yourselves together unto the supper of the great God;

The judgment of God upon those who fight against him appears to be the marriage supper, which is given to the birds.

18 That you may eat the flesh of kings, and the flesh of captains, and the flesh of mighty men, and the flesh of

horses, and of them that sit on them, and the flesh of all men, both free and bond, both small and great.

19 And I saw the beast, and the kings of the earth, and their armies, gathered together to make war against him that sat on the horse, and against his army.

This will be the gathering at Armageddon.

20 And the beast was taken, and with him the false prophet that wrought miracles before him, with which he deceived them that worshipped his image. These both were cast alive into a lake of fire burning with brimstone.

It is unclear whether the beast and false prophet represent people, spirits from the pit, or nations in this verse. The importance here is to realize, if these were people dying for the first time, they would go to a place of torment; but not to the second death, the lake of fire, which will be seen in Rev 20:10-15.

21 And the remnant were slain with the sword of him that sat upon the horse, which sword proceeded out of his mouth: and all the fowls were filled with their flesh.

The multitudes the angels influenced will die. Their cause of death will be hail stones on the great day of God's wrath. The hail will come after an earthquake has leveled the earth as mentioned in Rev 6:15-17.

Chapter 20

1   **And I saw an angel come down from heaven, having the key of the bottomless pit and a great chain in his hand.**

2   **And he laid hold on the dragon, that old serpent, which is the Devil, and Satan, and bound him a thousand years.**

3   **And cast him into the bottomless pit, and shut him up, and set a seal upon him, that he should deceive the nations no more, till the thousand years should be fulfilled: and after that he must be loosed a little season.**

In Chapter 9, Satan was given a key. With it, he released the angel of the bottomless pit. At this time, Satan will become one of the angels bound in the pit. However, just like the 4 angels bound at the Euphrates River, there will be a prophesied day of his release.

4   **And I saw thrones, and they sat upon them, and judgment was given unto them: and I saw the souls of them that were beheaded for the witness of Jesus, and for the word of God, and which had not worshipped the beast, neither his image, neither had received his mark upon their foreheads, or in their hands; and they lived and reigned with Christ a thousand years.**

5   **But the rest of the dead lived not again until the thousand years were finished. This is the first resurrection.**

Everyone who will be redeemed by God by the blood of Jesus will be made kings and priests as mentioned in Rev 5:9-10.

As explained in Chapter 13, there will be people who accept Jesus when the 144,000 are resurrected and caught up into heaven just after the great tribulation. Those who die for their faith during this period of the 2nd beast (the false prophet), will be brought back to life on earth and will reign with the rest of the redeemed. However, their spirits will not be able to enter into the throne room of God until the 7 vials have been poured out. These will be wedding guests at the marriage of the Lamb.

> **6 Blessed and holy is he that has part in the first resurrection: on such the second death has no power, but they shall be priests of God and of Christ, and shall reign with him a thousand years.**

After physical death, all people still have a spiritual life which lasts forever. Some lives will be tormented forever, but not those of the first resurrection. The first resurrection will consist of all who belong to Jesus.

In addition to the bride, friends of the bridegroom will be part of the first resurrection. The people who will accept Jesus after the 144,000 have risen plus the nation of Israel will be called friends of the bridegroom, the friends of Jesus. John 3:29 "He that has the bride is the bridegroom: but the friend of the bridegroom, which stands and hears him, rejoices greatly because of the bridegroom's voice..."

Both groups of spirits will be gathered together with Jesus. When Jesus returns to earth, their new bodies will be raised out of the earth. These spirits will then rejoin their new bodies on earth. Only the new bodies of Jesus and the 144,000 will have risen into heaven before the millennial reign of Jesus.

> **7 And when the thousand years are expired, Satan shall be loosed out of his prison,**
>
> **8 And shall go out to deceive the nations which are in the four quarters of the earth, Gog and Magog, to gather them together to battle: the number of whom is as the sand of the sea.**
>
> **9 And they went up on the breadth of the earth, and compassed the camp of the saints about, and the beloved city: and fire came down from God out of heaven, and devoured them.**

Jesus will likely rise into the air at the time Satan is set free. Those who belong to Jesus will be in and around Jerusalem, but multitudes from all over the earth will give themselves to Satan. Satan and his armies will once again fight against Jerusalem, but they will be defeated.

> **10 And the devil that deceived them was cast into the lake of fire and brimstone, where the beast and the false prophet are, and shall be tormented day and night for ever and ever.**

Since eternal beings can not be destroyed, God created the lake of fire. Matt 25:41 "...Depart from me, you cursed, into everlasting fire, prepared for the devil and his angels."

> **11 And I saw a great white throne, and him that sat on it, from whose face the earth and the heaven fled away; and there was found no place for them.**
> **12 And I saw the dead, small and great, stand before God; and the books were opened: and another book was opened, which is the book of life: and the dead were judged out of those things which were written in the books, according to their works.**
> **13 And the sea gave up the dead which were in it; and death and hell delivered up the dead which were in them: and they were judged every man according to their works.**
> **14 And death and hell were cast into the lake of fire. This is the second death.**
> **15 And whosoever was not found written in the book of life was cast into the lake of fire.**

There is no place in creation for those who resist God. Though they flee, they will be judged by God and cast into the lake of fire. This is metaphorically the outer darkness, the place separated from the light of God. Death will be defeated, and the spirits of all who have died will be judged. However, there will still be people who will be alive on the last day, when fire consumes the earth, when death is no more. 1 Cor 15:25-26 "For he must reign, till he has put all enemies under his feet. The last enemy that shall be destroyed is death."

The people who will be alive on the last day will be changed on that day. This will be the time shown in 1 Cor 15:51-54.

51 Behold, I show you a mystery; We shall not all sleep, but we shall all be changed,
52 In a moment, in the twinkling of an eye, at the last trump: for the trumpet shall sound, and the dead shall be raised incorruptible, and we shall be changed.
53 For this corruptible must put on incorruption, and this mortal must put on immortality.
54 So when this corruptible shall have put on incorruption, and this mortal shall have put on immortality, then shall be brought to pass the saying that is written, Death is swallowed up in victory.

The order of eternal life is given in 1 Cor 15:22-24.

22 For as in Adam all die, even so in Christ shall all be made alive.
23 But every man in his own order: Christ the firstfruits; afterward they that are Christ's at his coming.
24 Then comes the end, when he shall have delivered up the kingdom to God, even the Father; when he shall have put down all rule and all authority and power.

Verse 23 states that Jesus was the first to be resurrected. Not mentioned, the 144,000 will be the next group to be resurrected. When Jesus returns, the rest of the dead who belong to Jesus will be resurrected. Verse 24 states that once death is destroyed, Jesus will deliver all the rest who belong to him (both those who will die during the millennial kingdom and those who will still be alive on the last day), to the Father.

When the dead are raised at the end of the millennial kingdom, those who will be alive will be changed. 1 Thes 4:17 "Then we which are alive and remain (alive throughout the millennial kingdom will be changed and then) shall be caught up together with them (whose bodies will come out of the ground at the beginning of the millennial kingdom) in the clouds, to meet the Lord in the air: and so shall we ever be with the Lord (and we will all be delivered up in the air to Jesus, who will present us to the Father).

The last day of both heaven and earth is described. 2 Pet 3:12 "...the heavens being on fire shall be dissolved, and the elements shall melt with fervent heat..." Those who will be alive on this day will be saved through the fire, not from it, as foreshadowed in the third chapter of Daniel, especially verse 25. "...I see four men loose, walking in the midst of the fire, and they have no hurt; and the form of the fourth is like the Son of God."

Chapter 21

1 And I saw a new heaven and a new earth: for the first heaven and the first earth were passed away; and there was no more sea.

The signs of Jesus' coming are not part of the rest of this book, so commentary will be brief.

Just as some kernel of our bodies will be resurrected, heaven and earth will be a re-creation. In the new creation of earth there won't be any seas.

2 And I John saw the holy city, new Jerusalem, coming down from God out of heaven, prepared as a bride adorned for her husband.

This is similar to Rev 19:7 "Let us be glad and rejoice, and give honor to him: for the marriage of the Lamb is come, and his wife has made herself ready."

Christians, those of the 1st resurrection, will always have a special place, forever clothed as a bride.

3 And I heard a great voice out of heaven saying, Behold, the tabernacle of God is with men, and he will dwell with them, and they shall be his people, and God himself shall be with them, and be their God.

The eternal people of God from this present earth will join new people from a new Genesis. The new people will become the nations of the new earth. God will be with both mortal and eternal.

4 And God shall wipe away all tears from their eyes; and there shall be no more death, neither sorrow, nor crying, neither shall there be any more pain: for the former things are passed away.

5 And he that sat upon the throne said, Behold, I make all things new. And he said unto me, Write: for these words are true and faithful.

6 And he said unto me, It is done. I am Alpha and Omega, the beginning and the end. I will give unto him that is thirsty of the fountain of the water of life freely.

7 He that overcomes shall inherit all things; and I will be his God, and he shall be my son.

8 But the fearful, and unbelieving, and the abominable, and murderers, and whoremongers, and sorcerers, and idolaters, and all liars, shall have their part in the lake which burns with fire and brimstone: which is the second death.

9 And there came unto me one of the seven angels which had the seven vials full of the seven last plagues, and talked with me, saying, Come here, I will show you the bride, the Lamb's wife.

10 And he carried me away in the spirit to a great and high mountain, and showed me that great city, the holy Jerusalem, descending out of heaven from God.

11 Having the glory of God: and her light was like unto a stone most precious, even like a jasper stone, clear as crystal;

12 And had a wall great and high, and had twelve gates, and at the gates twelve angels, and names written thereon, which are the names of the twelve tribes of the children of Israel:

13 On the east three gates; on the north three gates; on the south three gates; and on the west three gates.

14 And the wall of the city had twelve foundations, and in them the names of the twelve apostles of the Lamb.

15 And he that talked with me had a golden reed to measure the city, and the gates thereof, and the wall thereof.

16 And the city lies foursquare, and the length is as large as the breadth: and he measured the city with the reed, twelve thousand furlongs. The length and the breadth and the height of it are equal.

17 And he measured the wall thereof, an hundred and forty and four cubits, according to the measure of a man, that is, of an angel.

18 And the building of the wall of it was of jasper: and the city was pure gold, like unto clear glass.

19 And the foundations of the wall of the city were garnished with all manner of precious stones. The first foundation was jasper; the second, sapphire; the third, a chalcedony; the fourth, an emerald;

20 The fifth, sardonyx; the sixth, sardius; the seventh, chrysolyte; the eighth, beryl; the ninth, a topaz; the tenth, a chrysoprasus; the eleventh, a jacinth; the twelfth, an amethyst.

21 And the twelve gates were twelve pearls: every several gate was of one pearl: and the street of the city was pure gold, as it were transparent glass.

22 And I saw no temple therein: for the Lord God Almighty and the Lamb are the temple of it.

23 And the city had no need of the sun, neither of the moon, to shine in it: for the glory of God did lighten it, and the Lamb is the light thereof.

Pictured is a crystal pyramid. In the midst of its base is the pure light of God being refracted into the multitude of listed colors. The gates must be round because the pearls are the pure white light of God flowing out of them.

24 And the nations of them which are saved shall walk in the light of it: and the kings of the earth do bring their glory and honor into it.

25 And the gates of it shall not be shut at all by day: for there shall be no night there.

26 And they shall bring the glory and honor of the nations into it.

This crystal pyramid will exist as a city on the new earth. Many other cities will also exist among the nations.

27 And there shall in no wise enter into it any thing that defiles, neither whatsoever works abomination, or makes a lie: but they which are written in the Lamb's book of life.

Chapter 22

1 And he showed me a pure river of water of life, clear as crystal, proceeding out of the throne of God and of the Lamb.

The "pure river of water of life" is a picture of the Holy Spirit.

2 In the midst of the street of it, and on either side of the river, was there the tree of life, which bare twelve manners of fruits, and yielded her fruit every month: and the leaves of the tree were for the healing of the nations.

The 2 trees may refer to the 2 witnesses, the 144,000 from the 12 tribes of Israel. They may still be witnesses in the new creation.

3 And there shall be no more curse: but the throne of God and of the Lamb shall be in it; and his servants shall serve him:

It may not be possible for sin to enter this new earth as it did in the once sinless earth of Genesis.

4 And they shall see his face; and his name shall be in their foreheads.
5 And there shall be no night there; and they need no candle, neither light of the sun; for the Lord God gives them light: and they shall reign for ever and ever.

Since all of creation groans, it will probably all be renewed in a manner similar to what it is now. However, God's light will always shine in Jerusalem. God's bride of Rev 19:9 will reign over the new nations of the new earth forever.

Aren't you glad you are a Christian! What great promises have been given to us, in Chapters 2 and 3, and in this section!

6 And he said unto me, These sayings are faithful and true: and the Lord God of the holy prophets sent his angel to show unto his servants the things which must shortly be done.

7 Behold, I come quickly: blessed is he that keeps the sayings of the prophecy of this book.

8 And I John saw these things, and heard them. And when I had heard and seen, I fell down to worship before the feet of the angel which showed me these things.

9 Then he said to unto me, See you do it not; for I am your fellow servant, and of your brethren the prophets, and of them which keep the saying of this book: worship God.

10 And he said unto me, Seal not the saying of the prophecy of this book: for the time is at hand.

11 He that is unjust, let him be unjust still: and he which is filthy, let him be filthy still: and he that is righteous, let him be righteous still: and he that is holy, let him be holy still.

12 And, behold, I come quickly; and my reward is with me, to give every man according as his work shall be.

13 I am Alpha and Omega, the beginning and the end, the first and the last.

14 Blessed are they that do his commandments, that they may have the right to the tree of life, and may enter in through the gates into the city.

15 For without are dogs, and sorcerers, and whoremongers, and murderers, and idolaters, and whosoever loves and makes a lie.

16 I Jesus have sent my angel to testify unto you these things in the churches. I am the root and the offspring of David, and the bright and morning star.

17 And the Spirit and the bride say, Come. And let him that hears say, Come. And let him that is thirsty come. And whosoever will, let him take the water of life freely.

The Spirit of God says "Come." Christians say "Come." Those who are guided by the Spirit of God say "Come." Those who want the promises of God to Christians, "Come," the Spirit of God is a gift!

18 For I testify unto every man that hears the words of the prophecy of this book, If any man shall add unto these things, God shall add unto him the plagues that are written in this book;

19 And if any man shall take away from the words of the book of this prophecy, God shall take away his part out of the book of life, and out of the holy city, and from the things which are written in this book.

20 He which testifies these things says, Surely I come quickly. Amen. Even so, come, Lord Jesus.

21 The grace of our Lord Jesus Christ be with you all. Amen.

Appendix 1

Defined Symbols

1:20	7 stars = 7 angels of the 7 churches 1:20
1:20	7 candlesticks = 7 churches
3:12	Name of the city of God = new Jerusalem
4:5	7 lamps of fire burning before the throne = 7 Spirits of God
5:6	7 horns and 7 eyes of the Lamb = 7 Spirits of God
5:8	Odors in golden vials = prayers of the saints
12:9	Great dragon = that old serpent, called the Devil and Satan Also 20:2
17:9	7 heads = 7 mountains on which the woman sits
17:10	7 heads = 7 kings, 5 were dead, 1 was alive when John wrote, and when the 7th king comes, he won't last long
17:12	10 horns = 10 kings that were not in power when John wrote
17:15	The waters where the whore sits = peoples, and multitudes, and nations, and tongues
17:18	The woman = the great city which reigns over the kings of the earth
19:8	Bride clothes - Fine linen, clean and white = the righteousness of saints Compare 7:14 Robes are made white in the blood of the Lamb